Barking in Disguise

A Funny Picture Book of Dogs in Costumes

The adorable and funny faces in this picture book were brought to life with the creative assistance of AI, capturing the playful spirit of these animals in a whole new way.

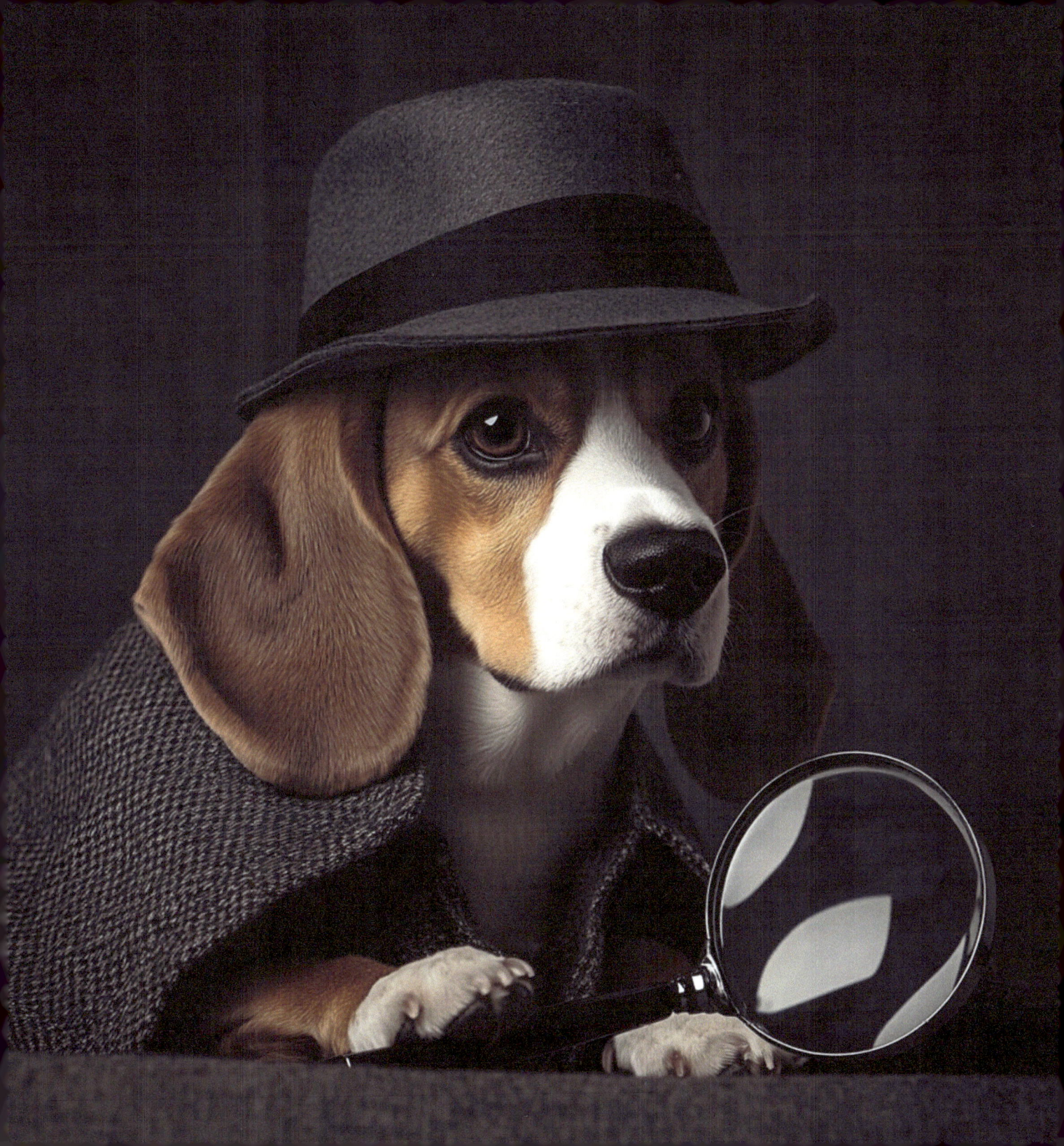

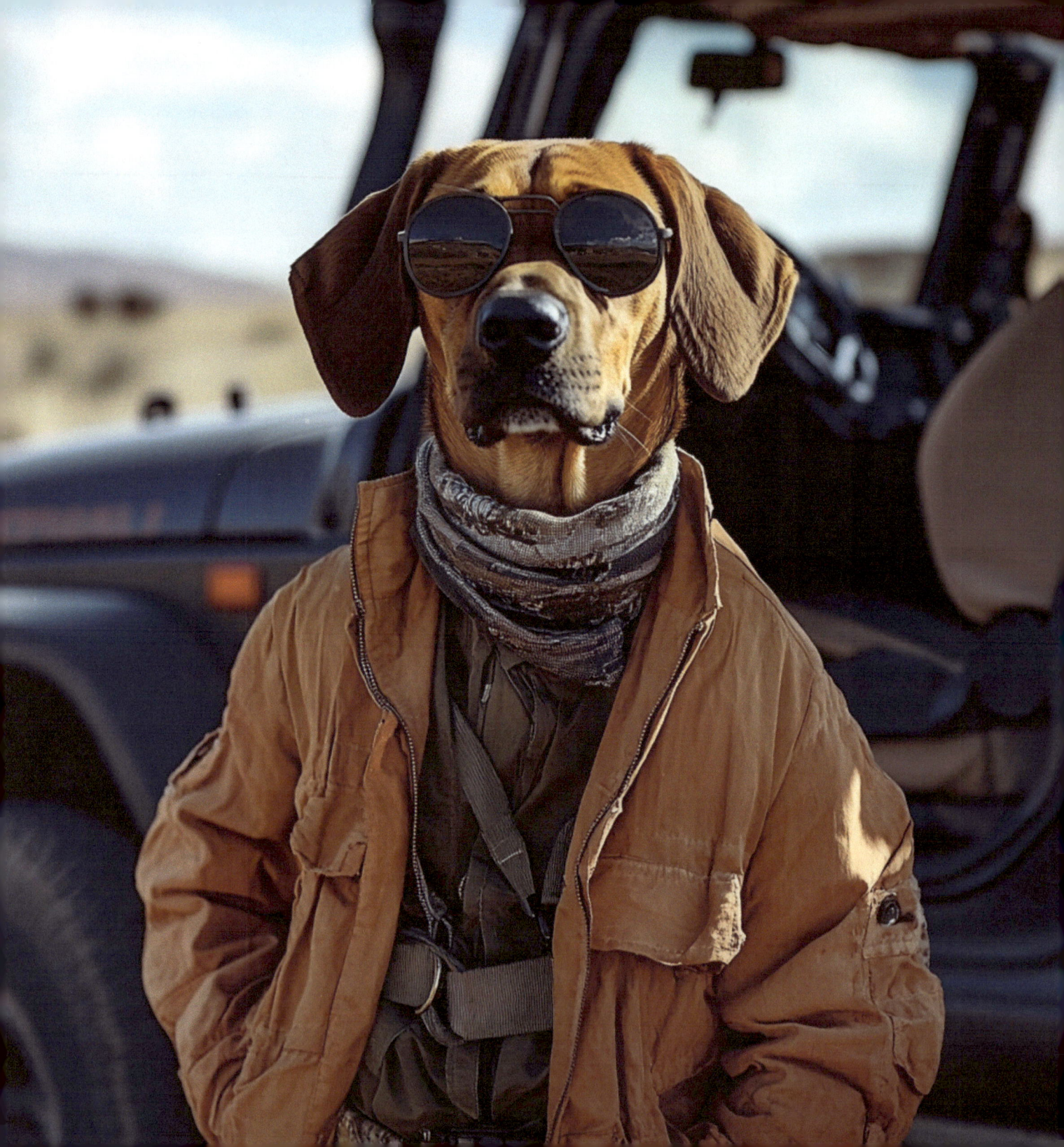

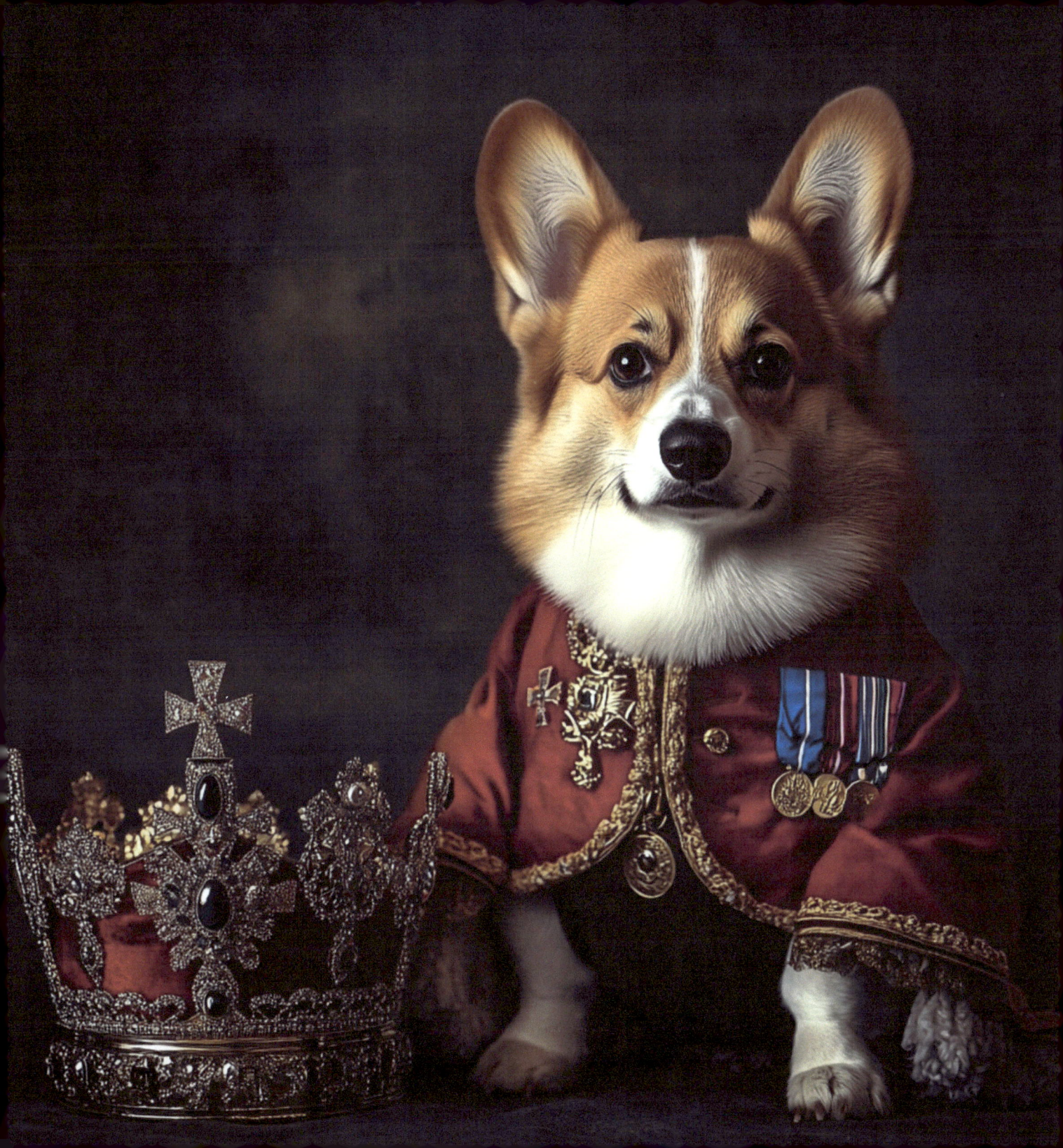

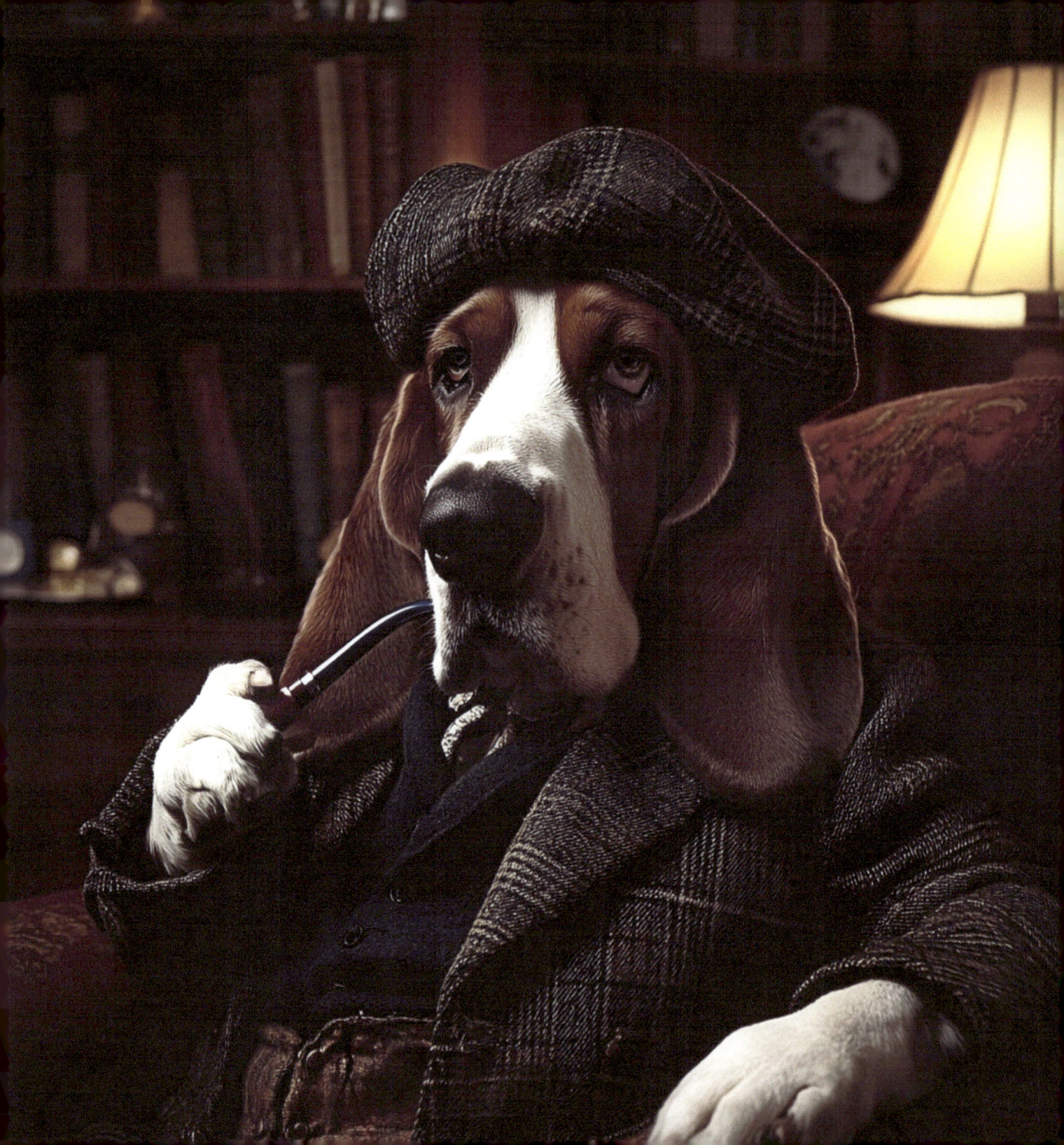

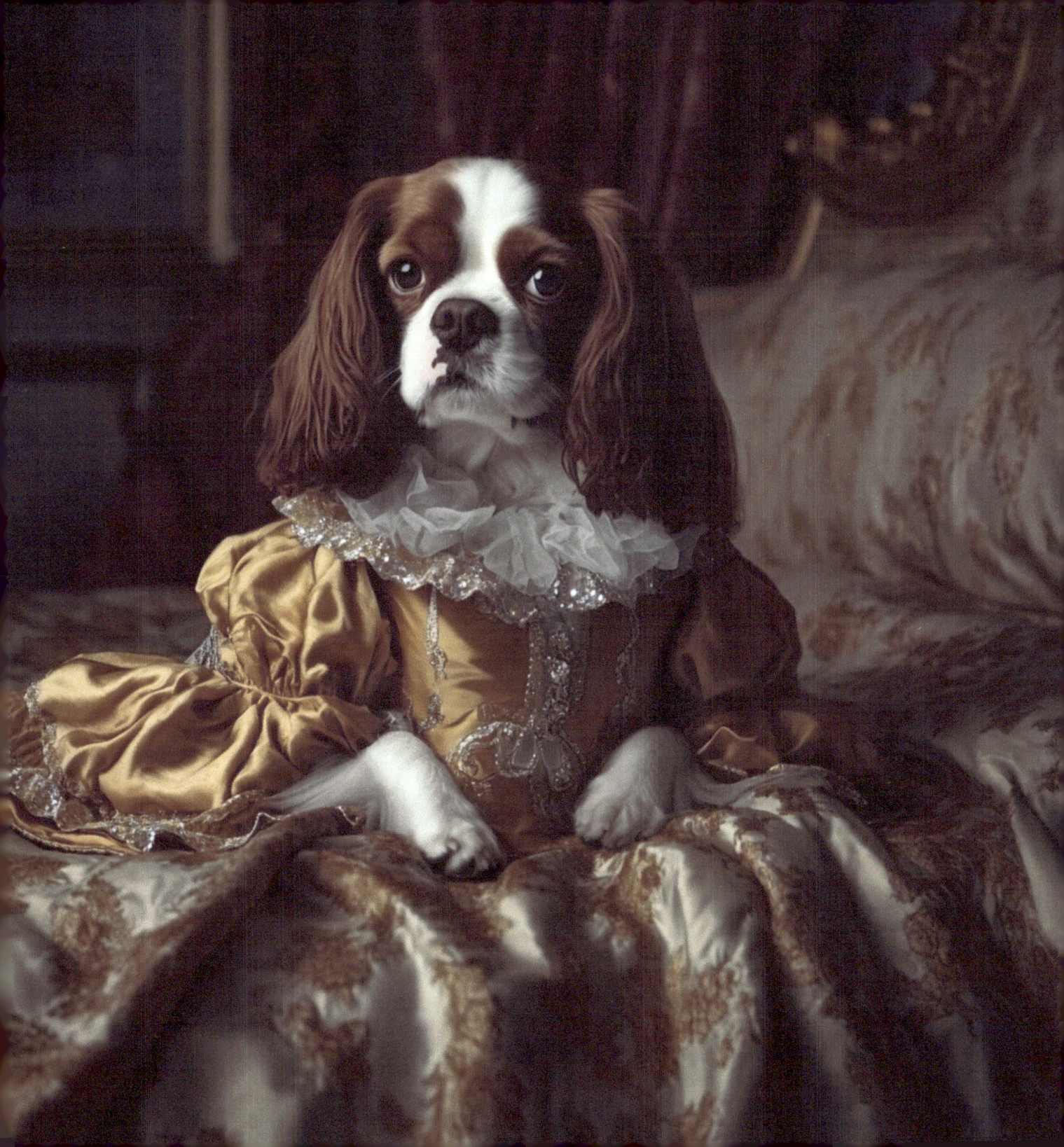

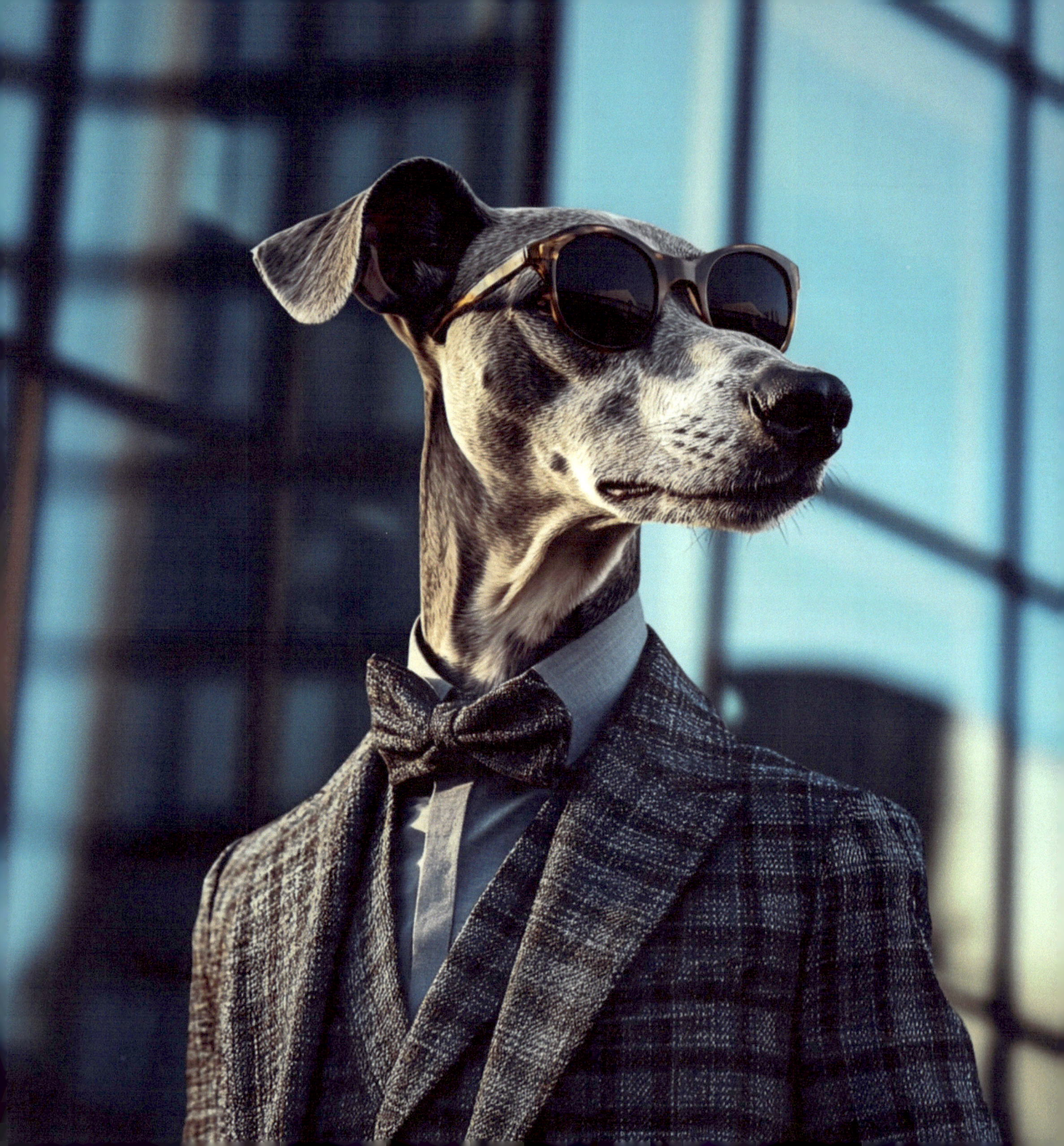

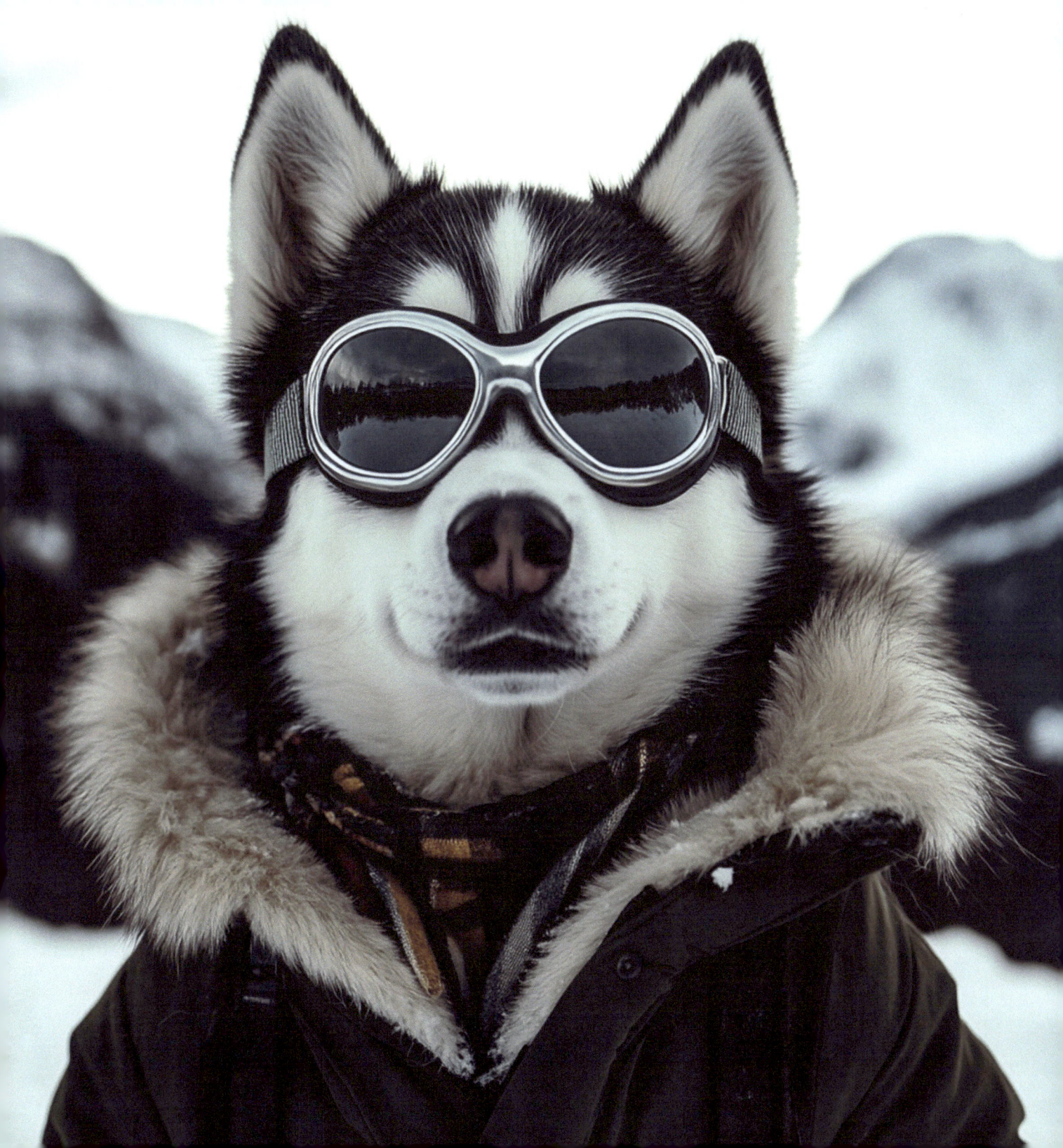

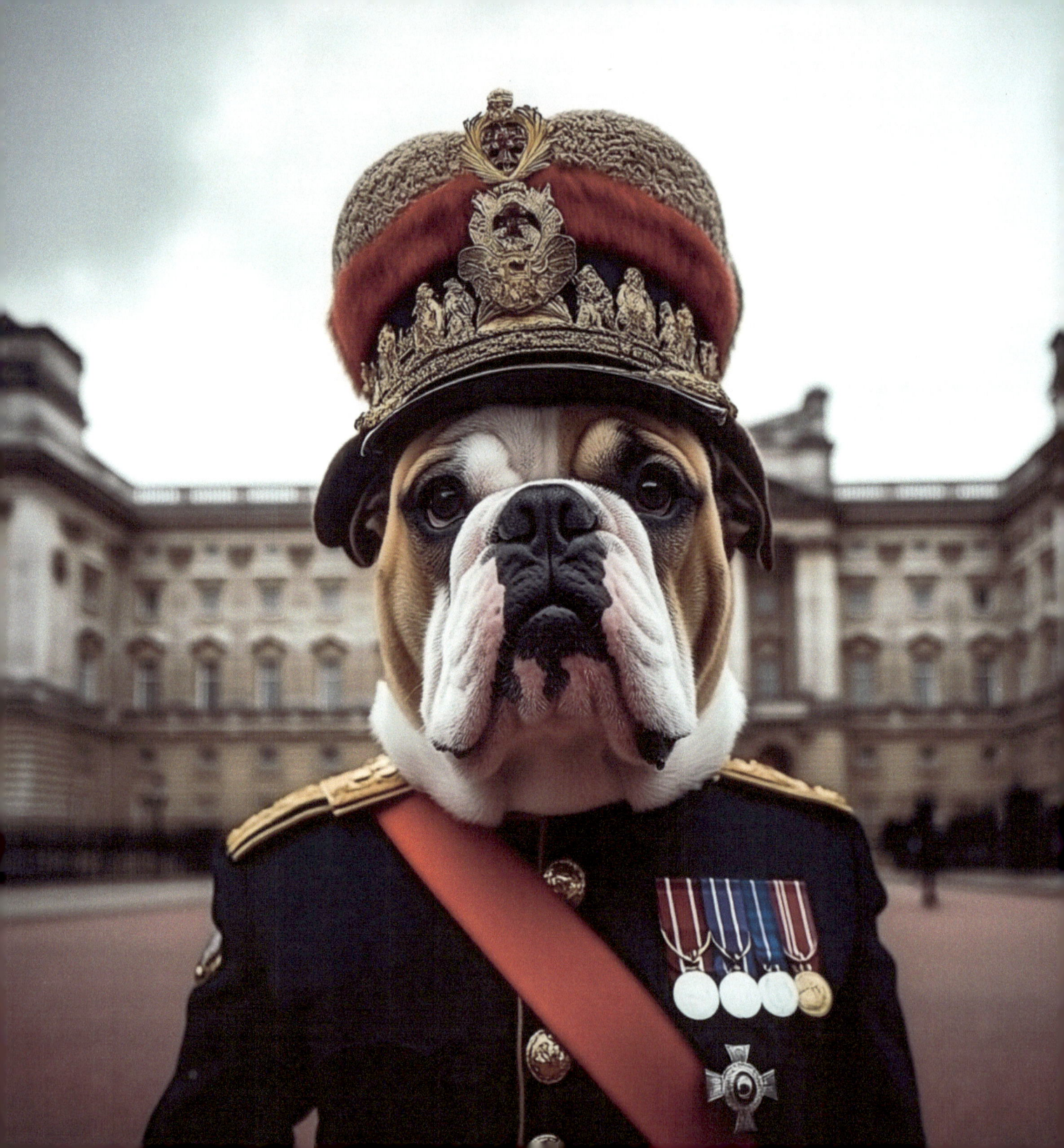

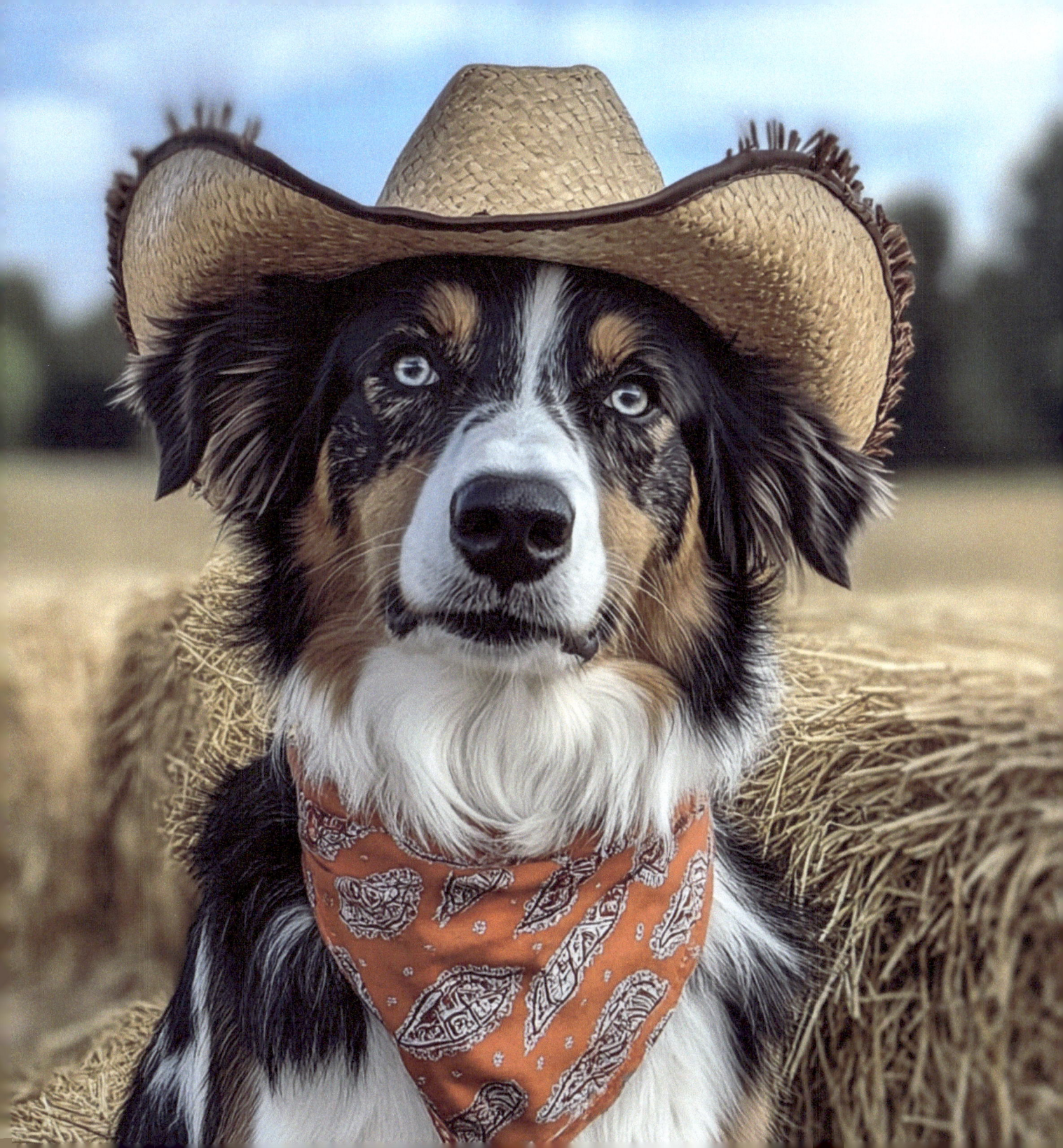

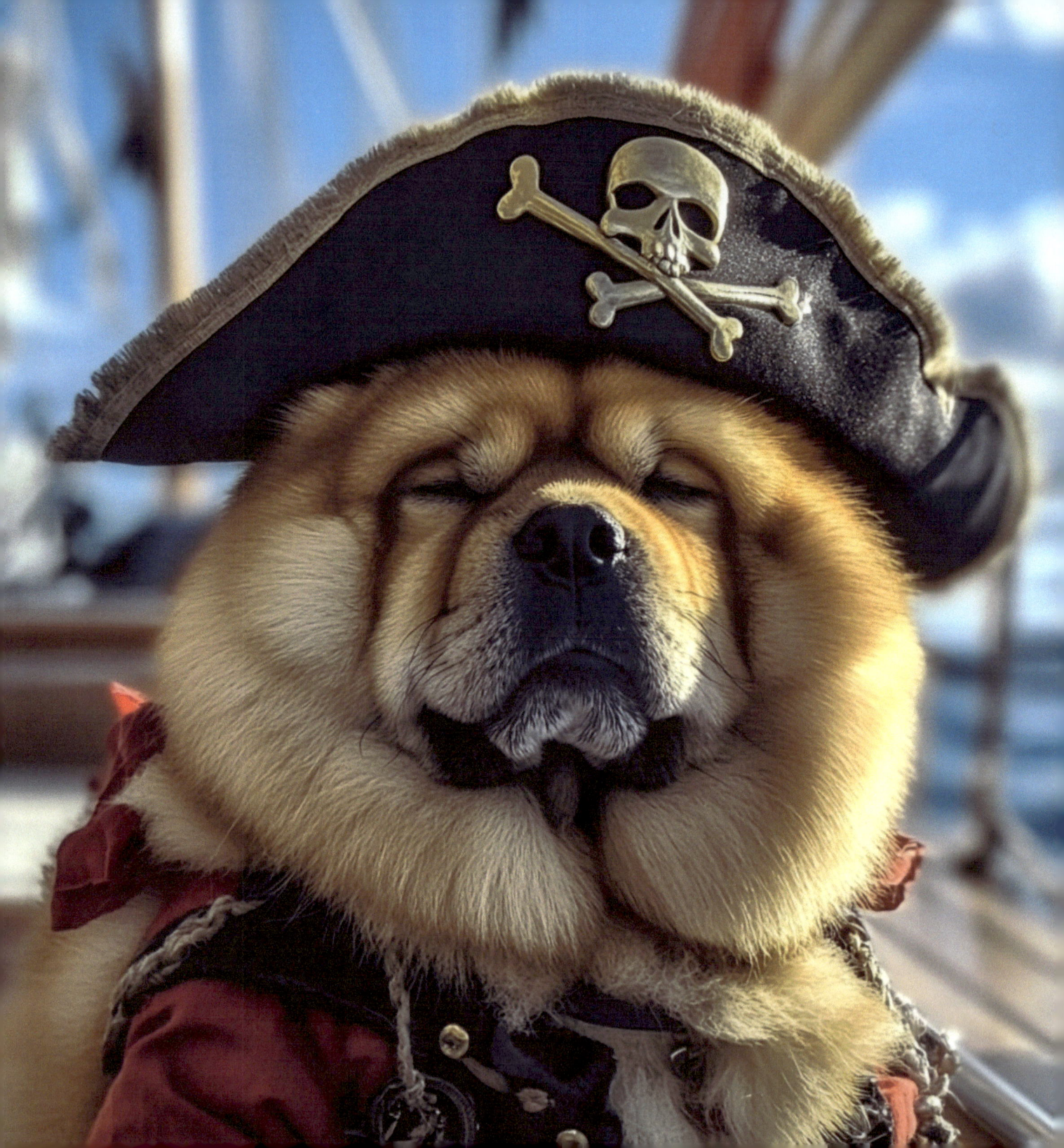

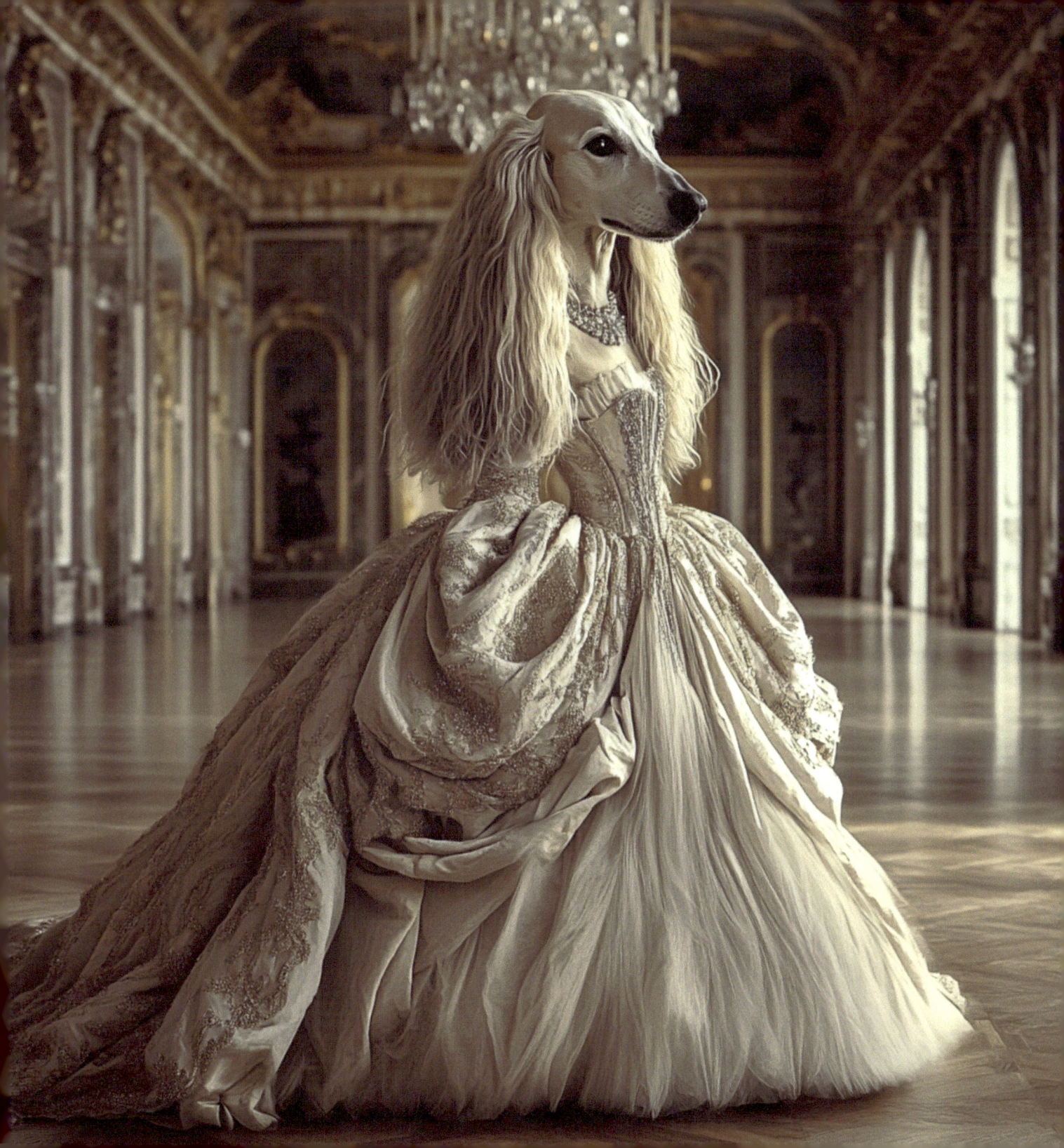

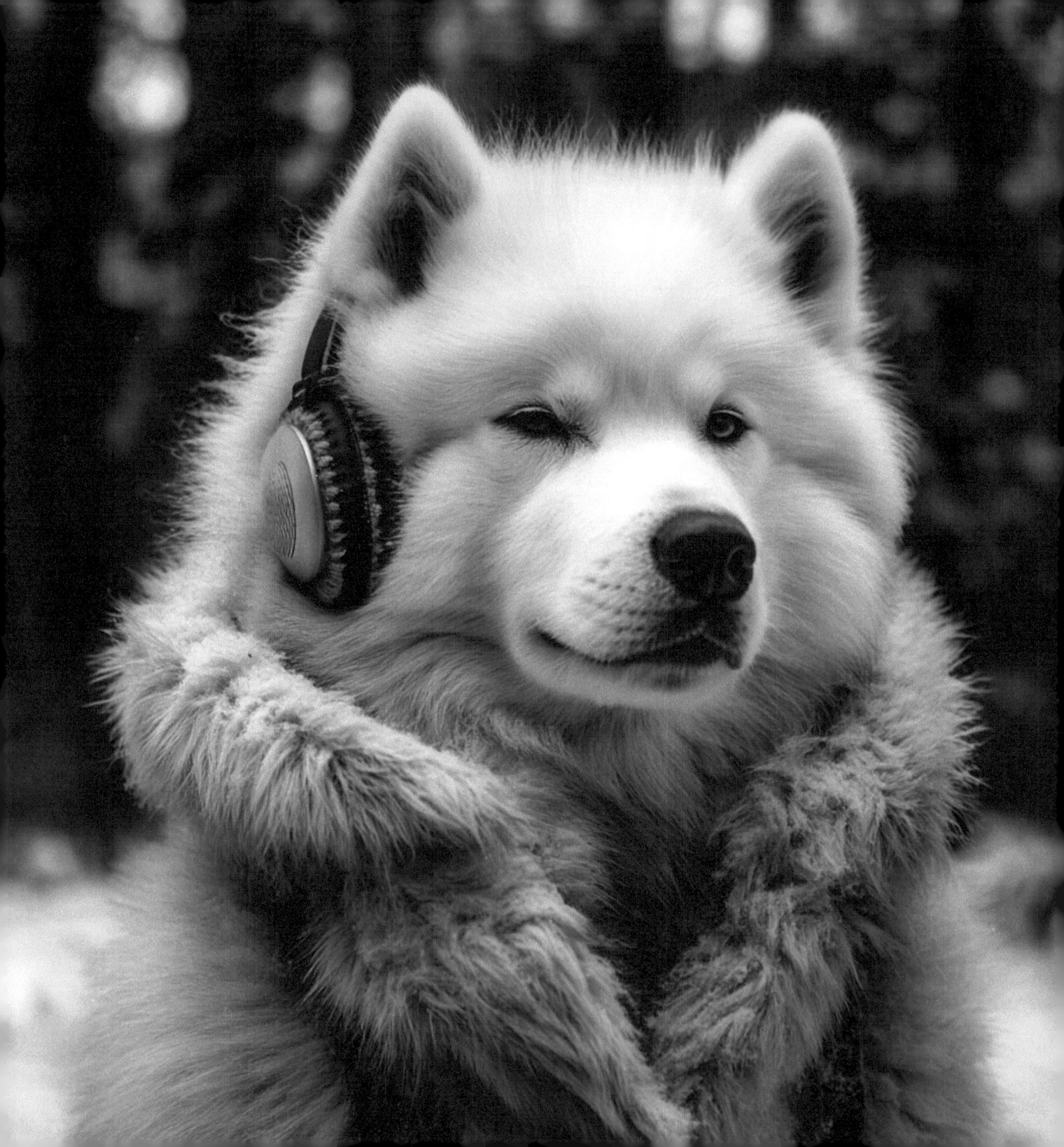

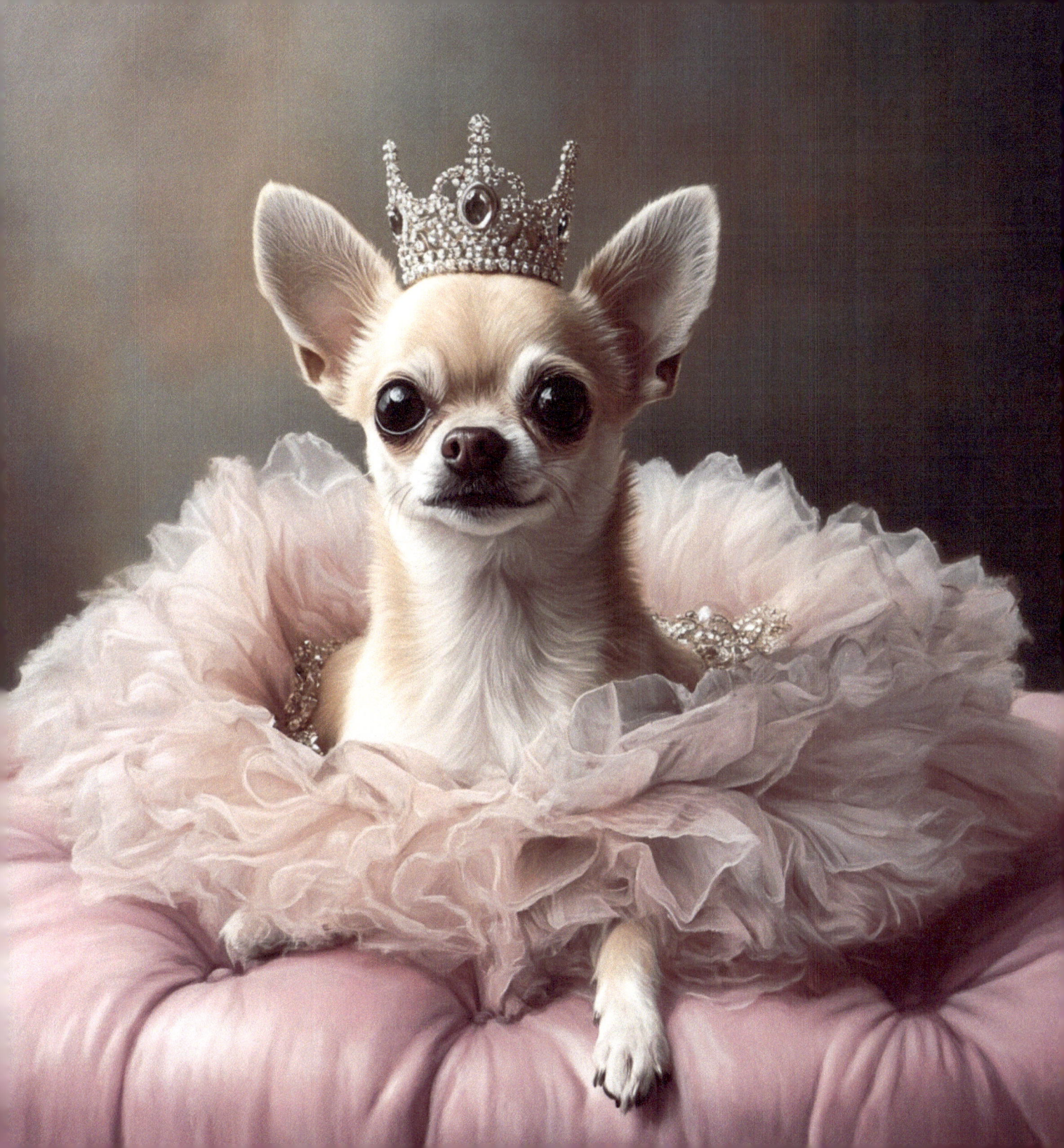

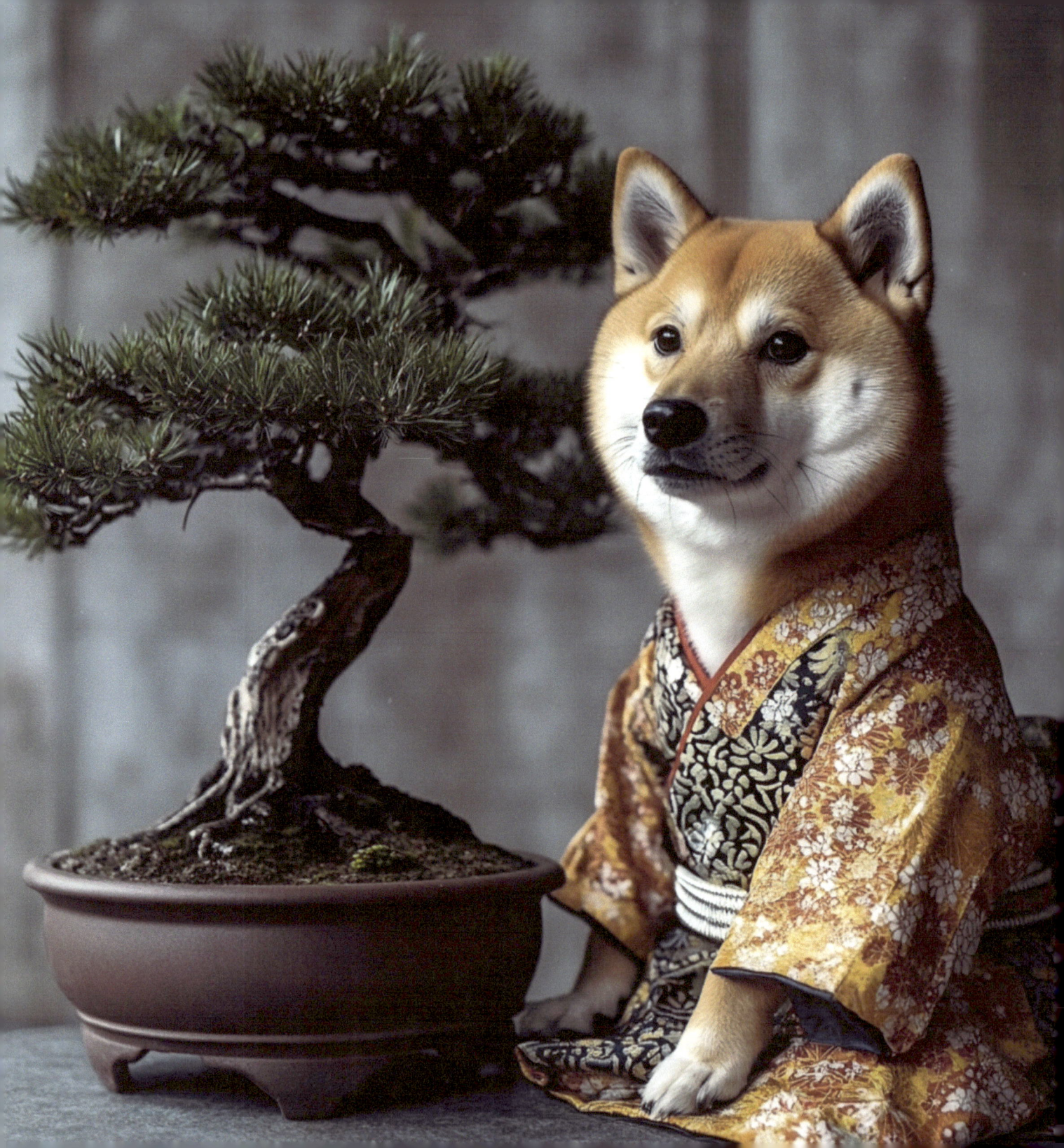

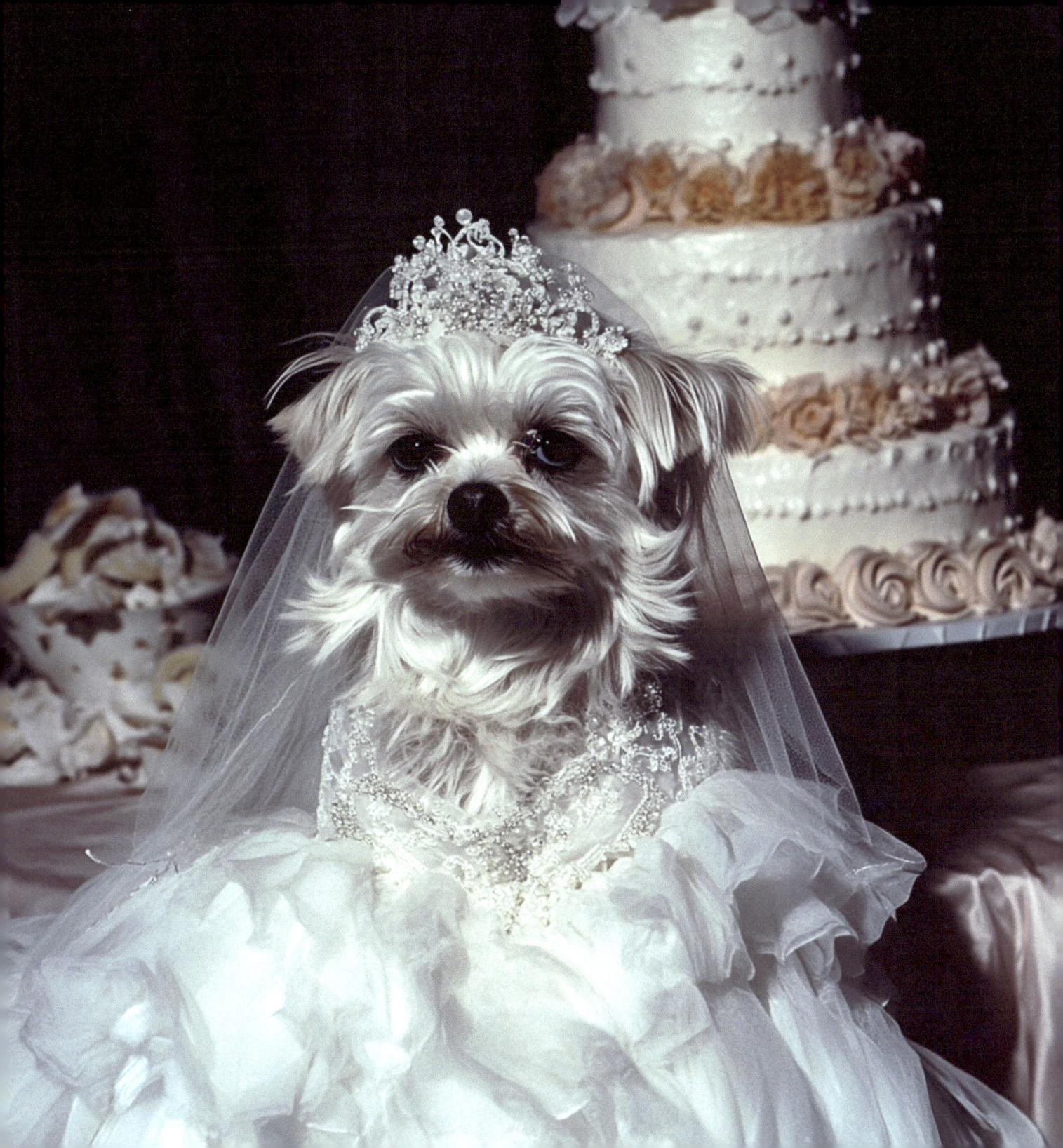

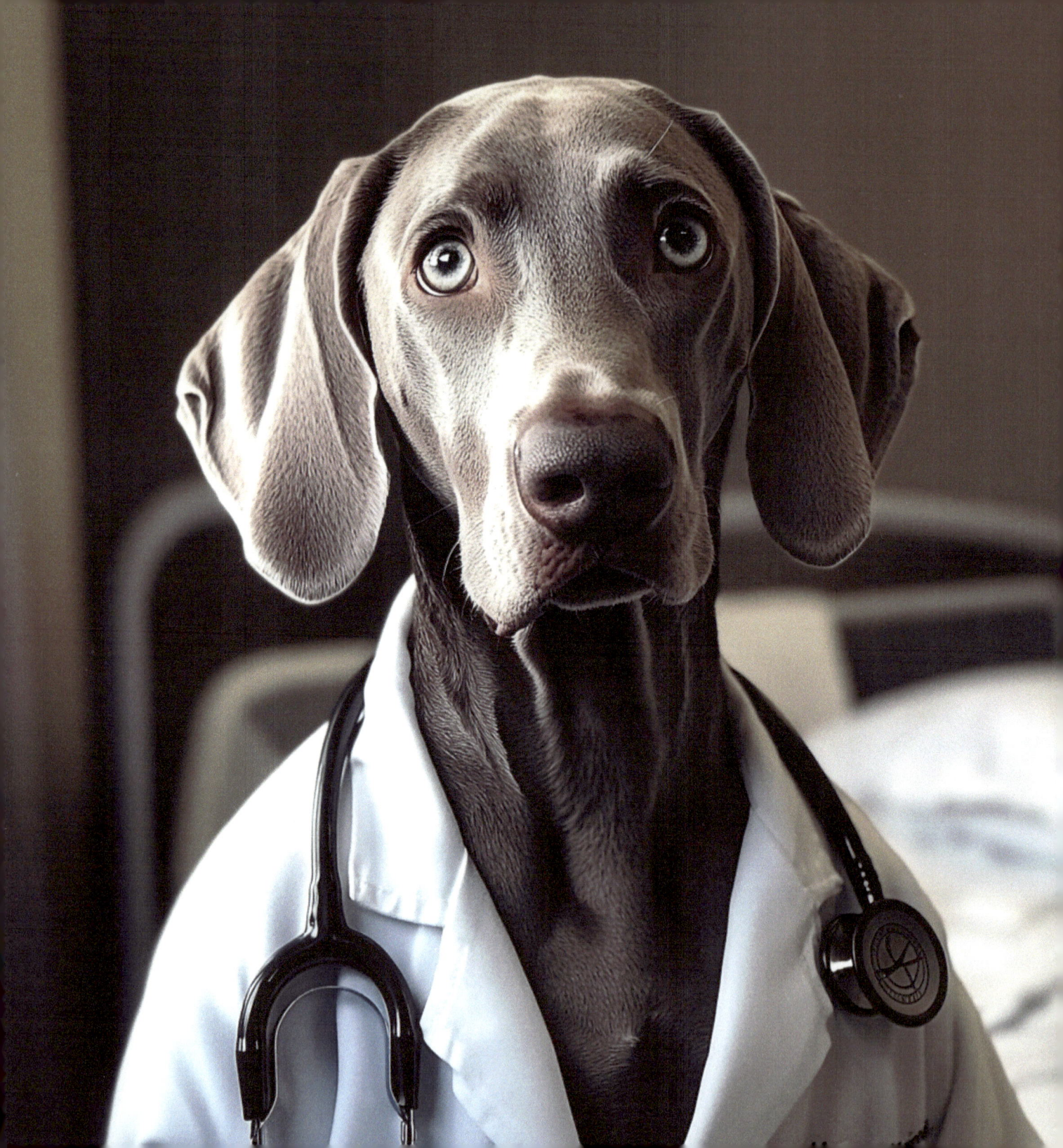

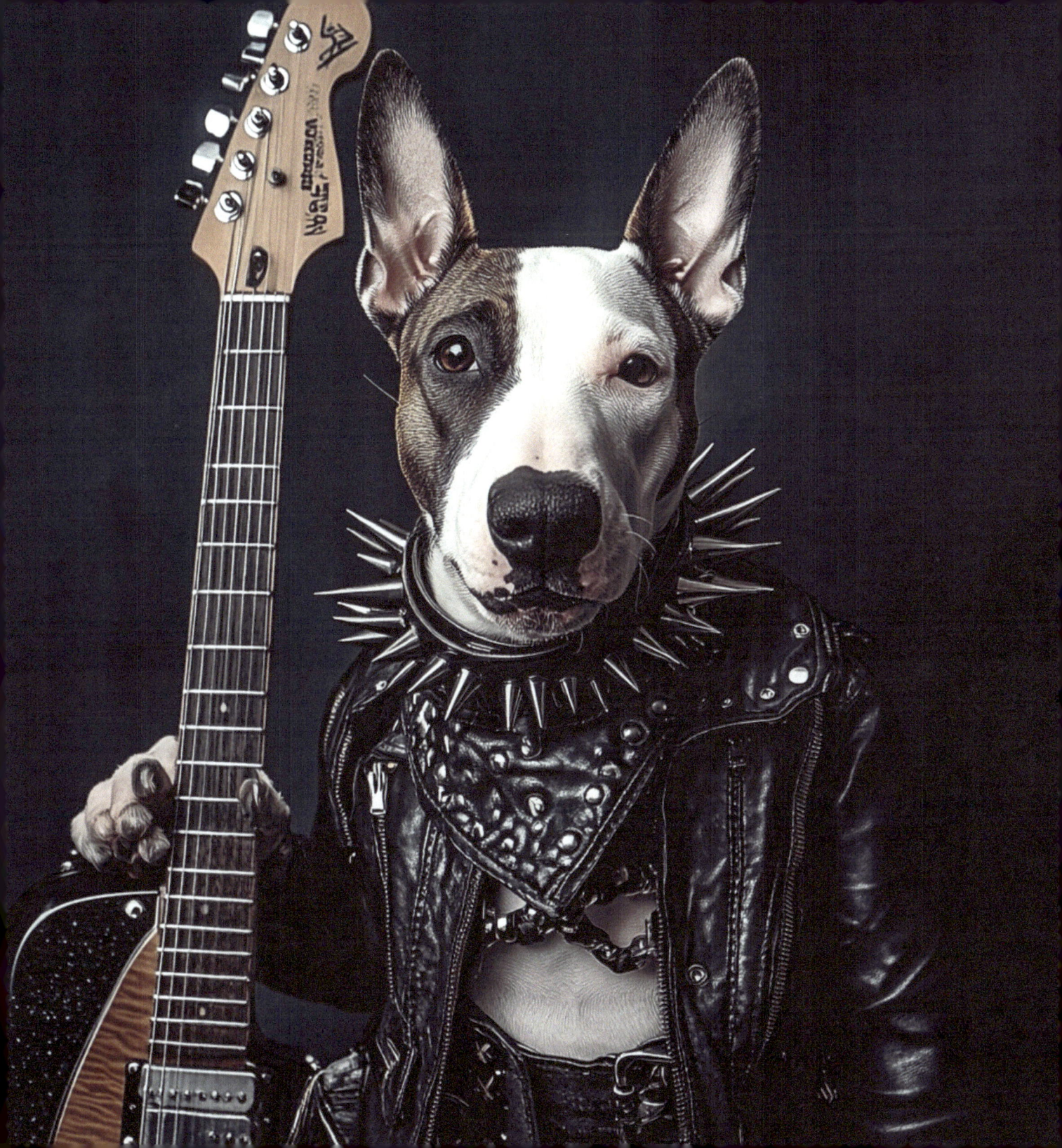

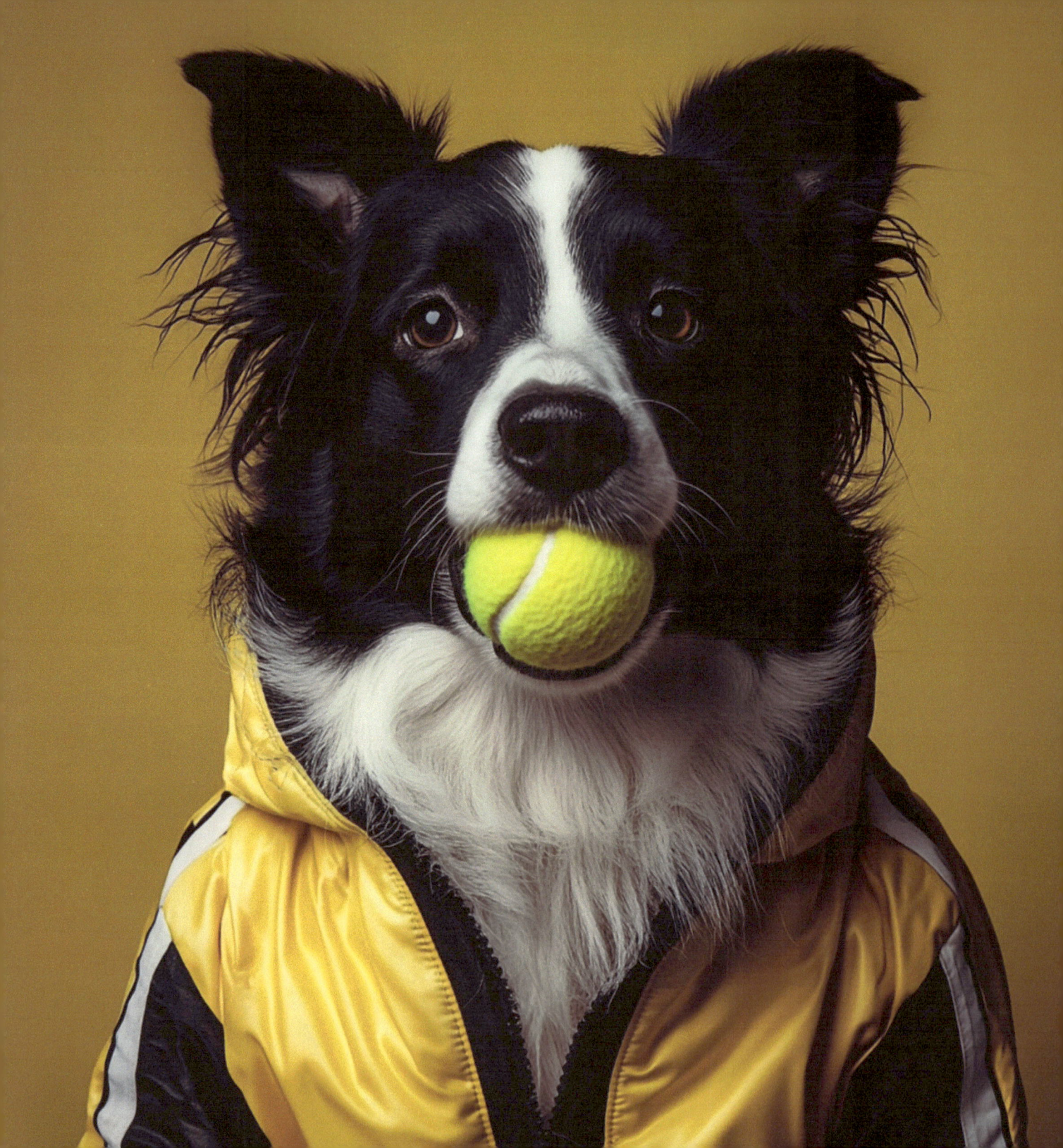

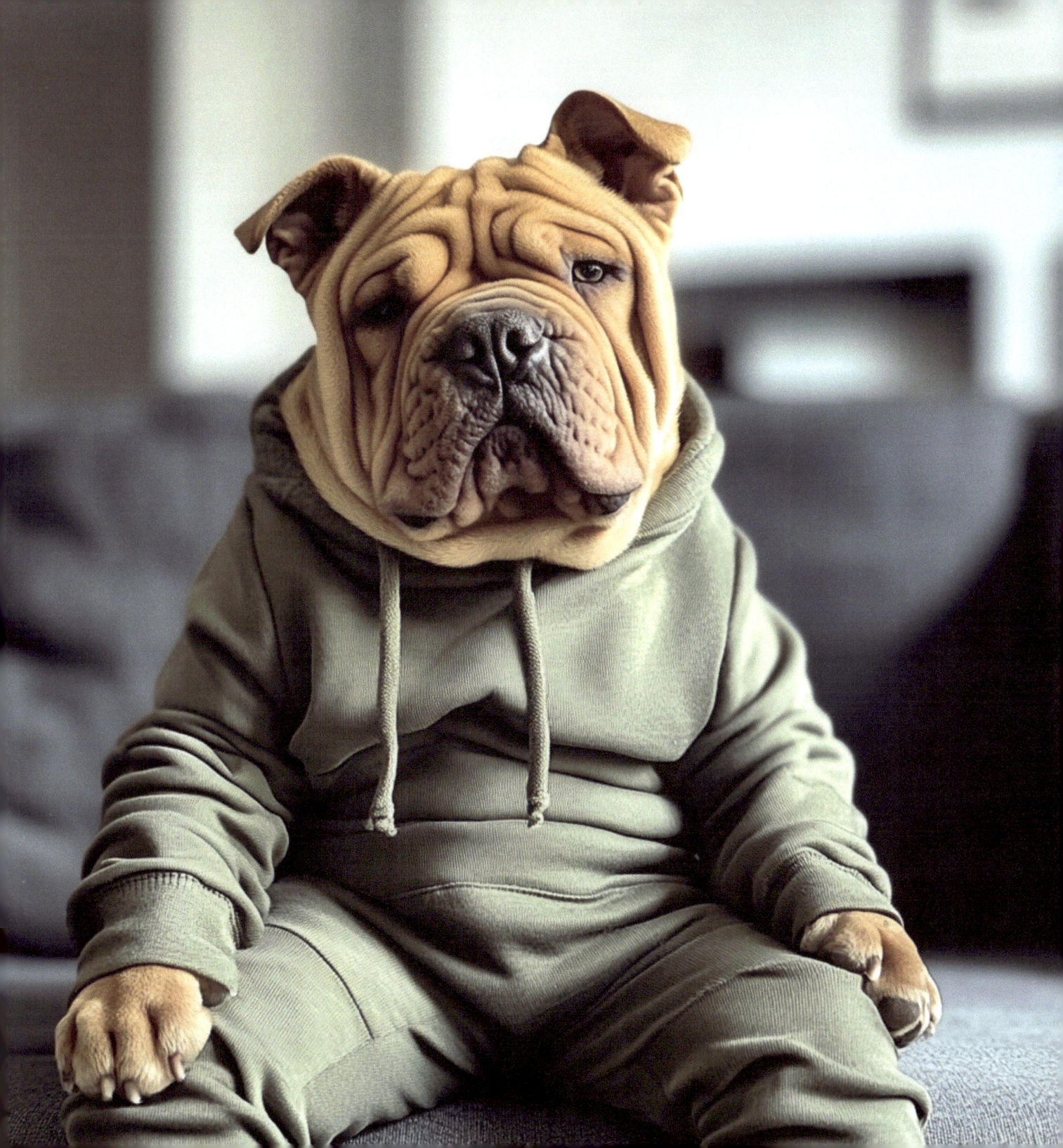

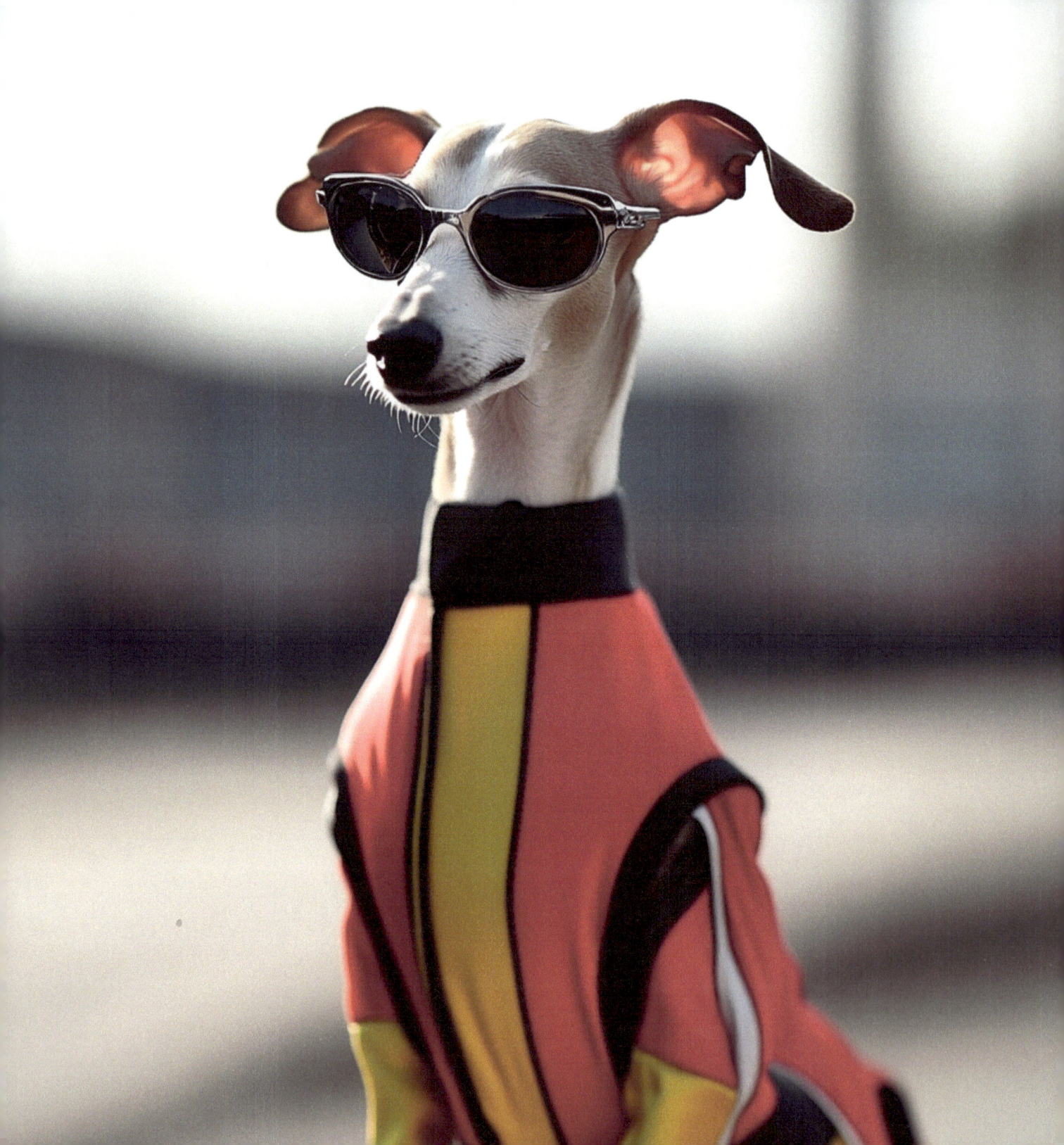

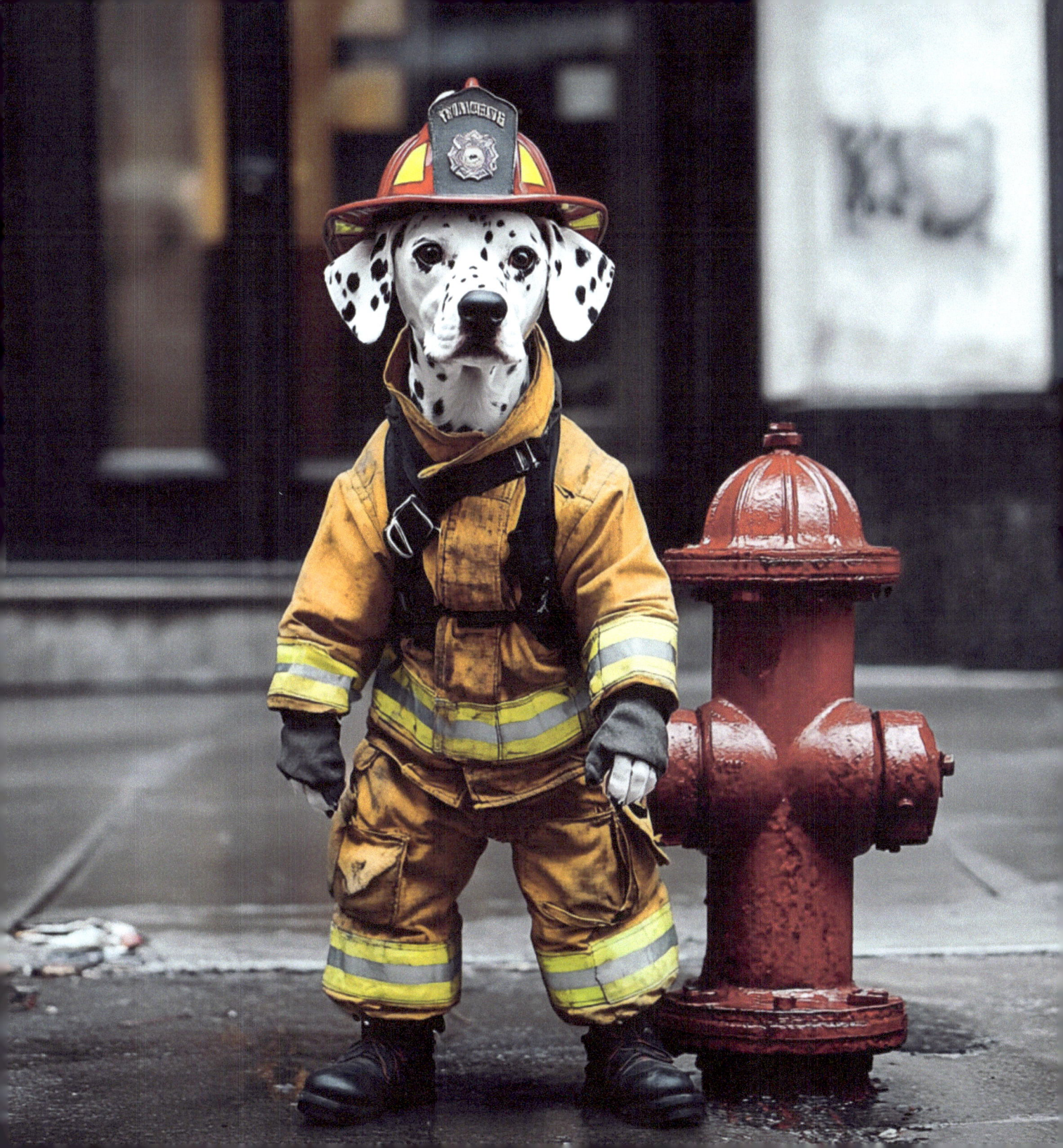

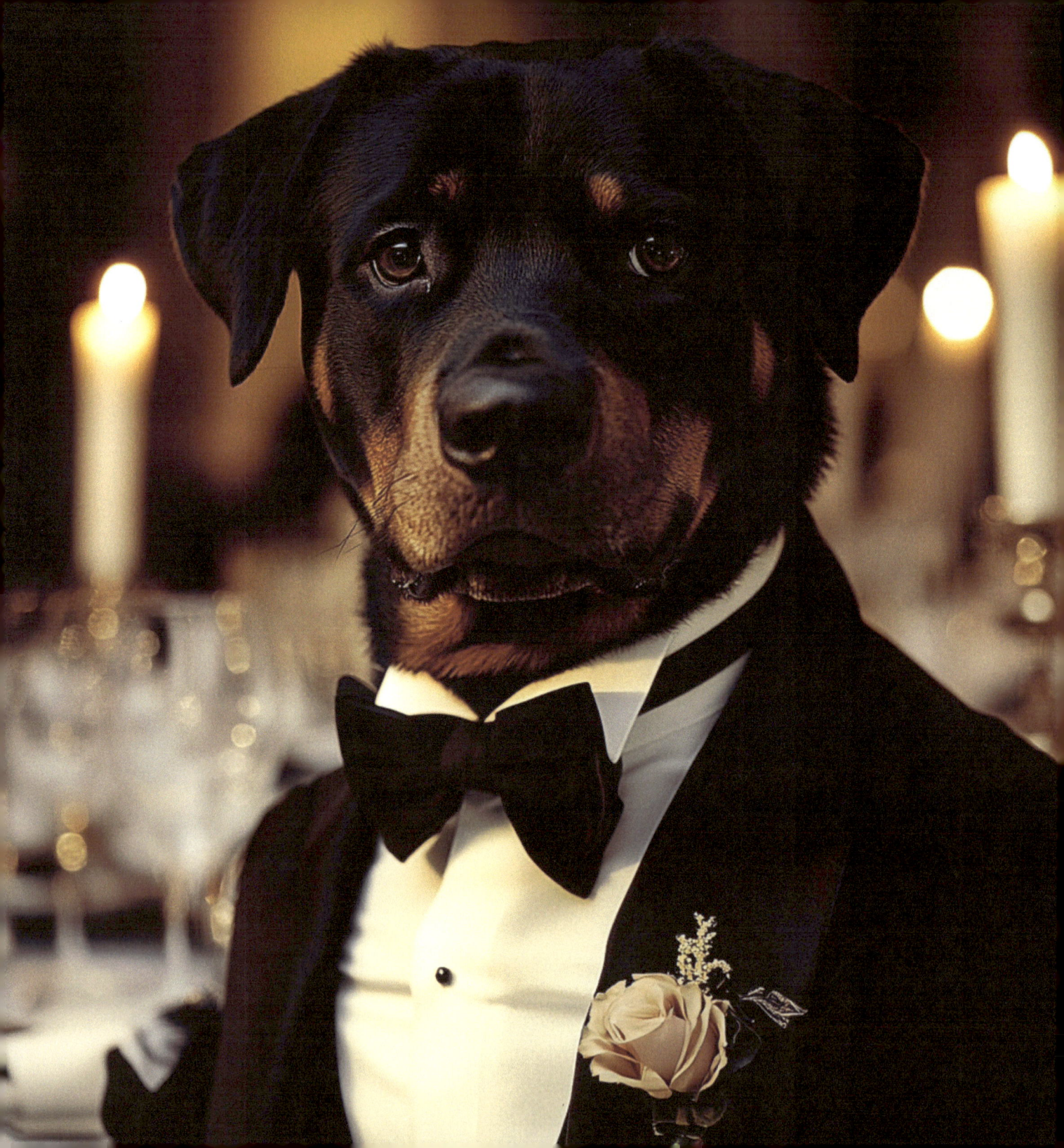

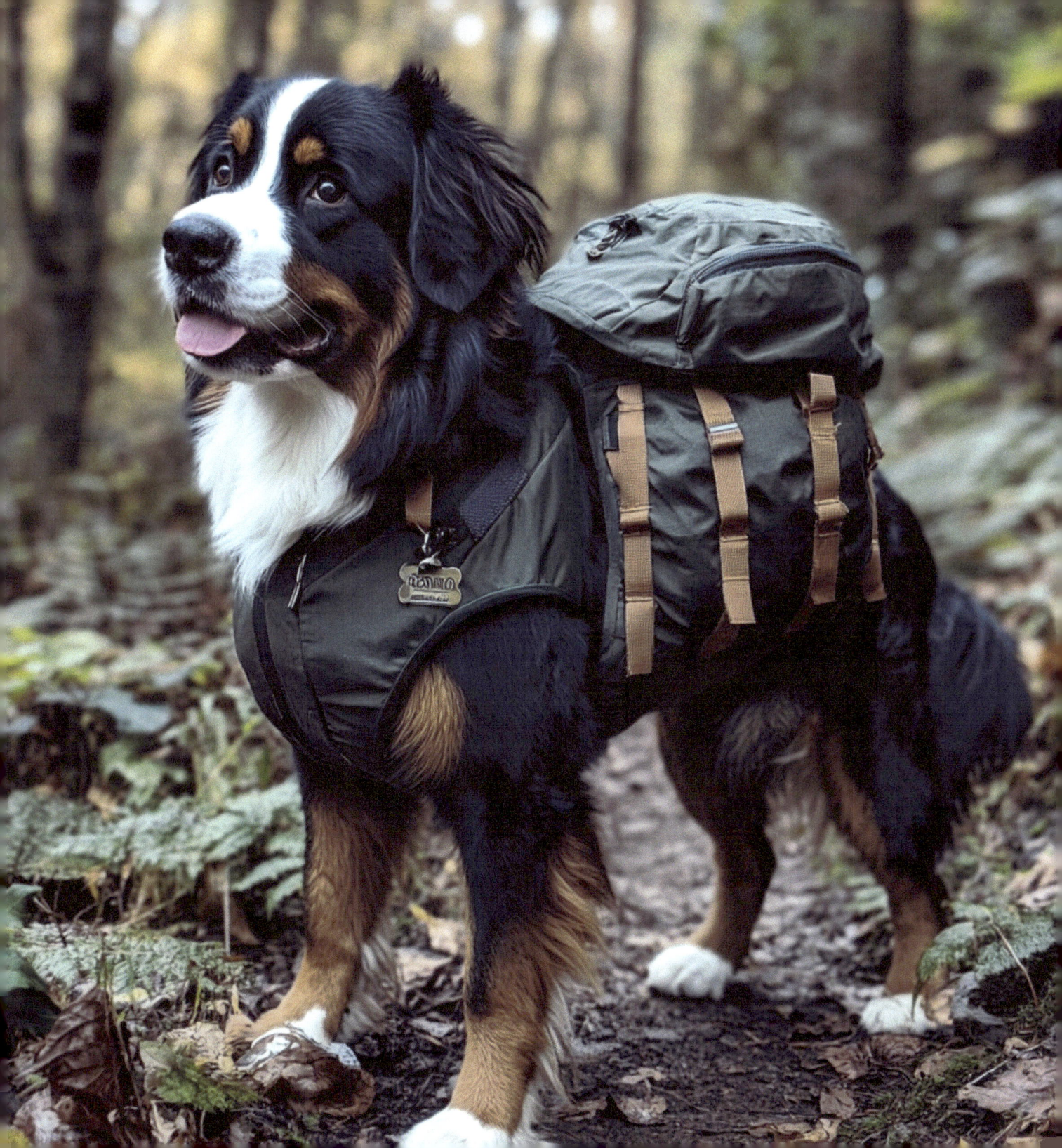

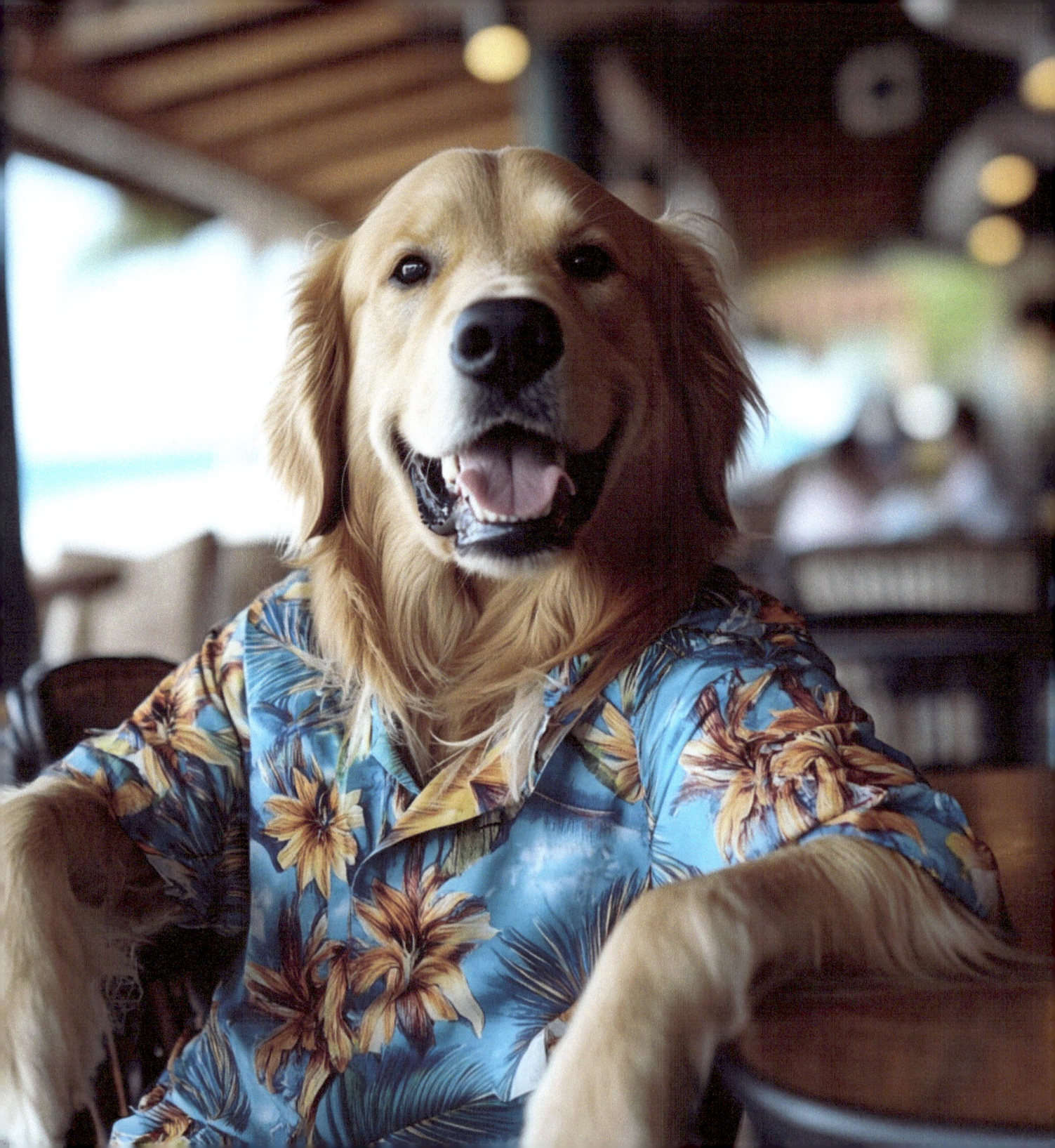

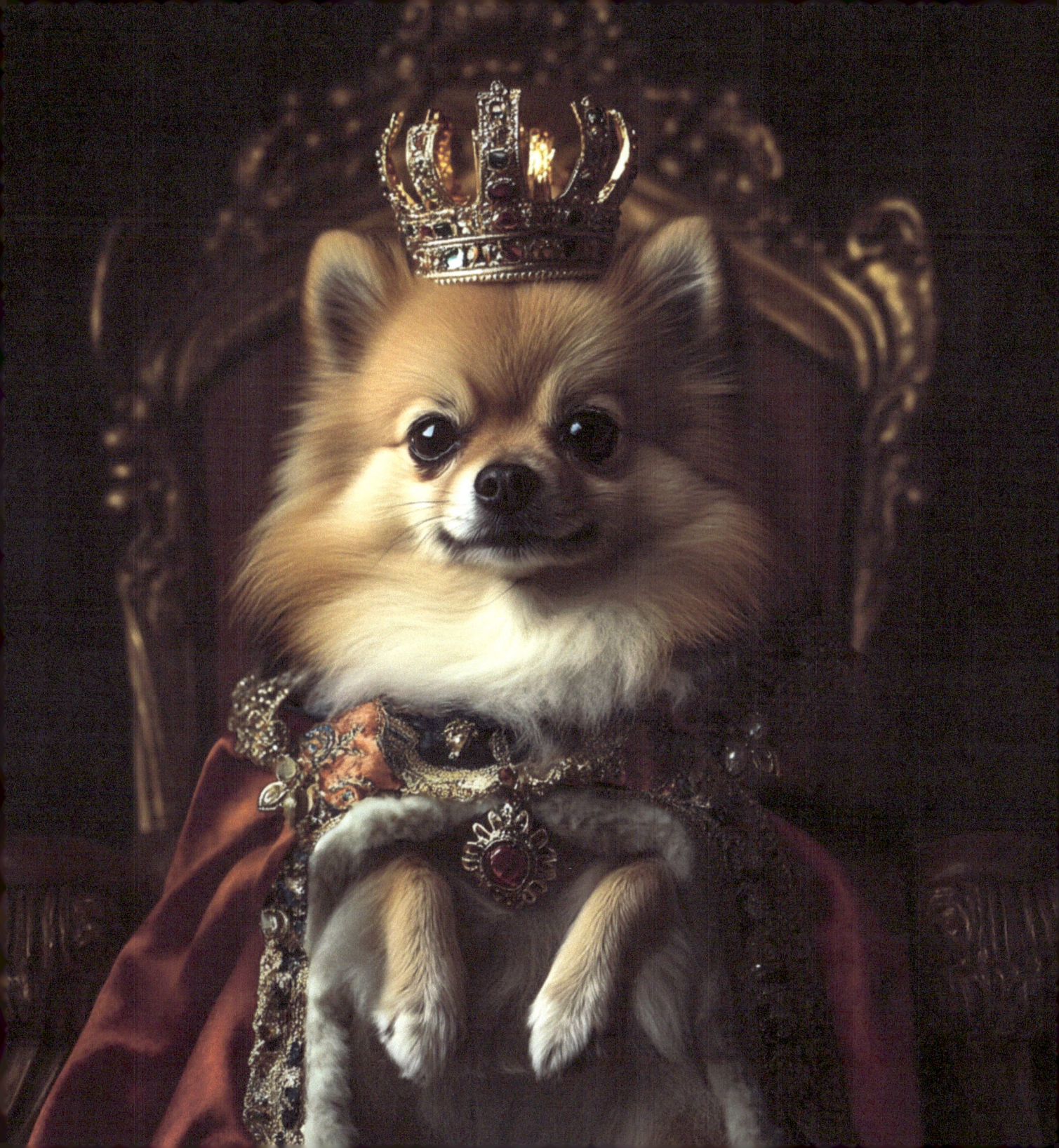

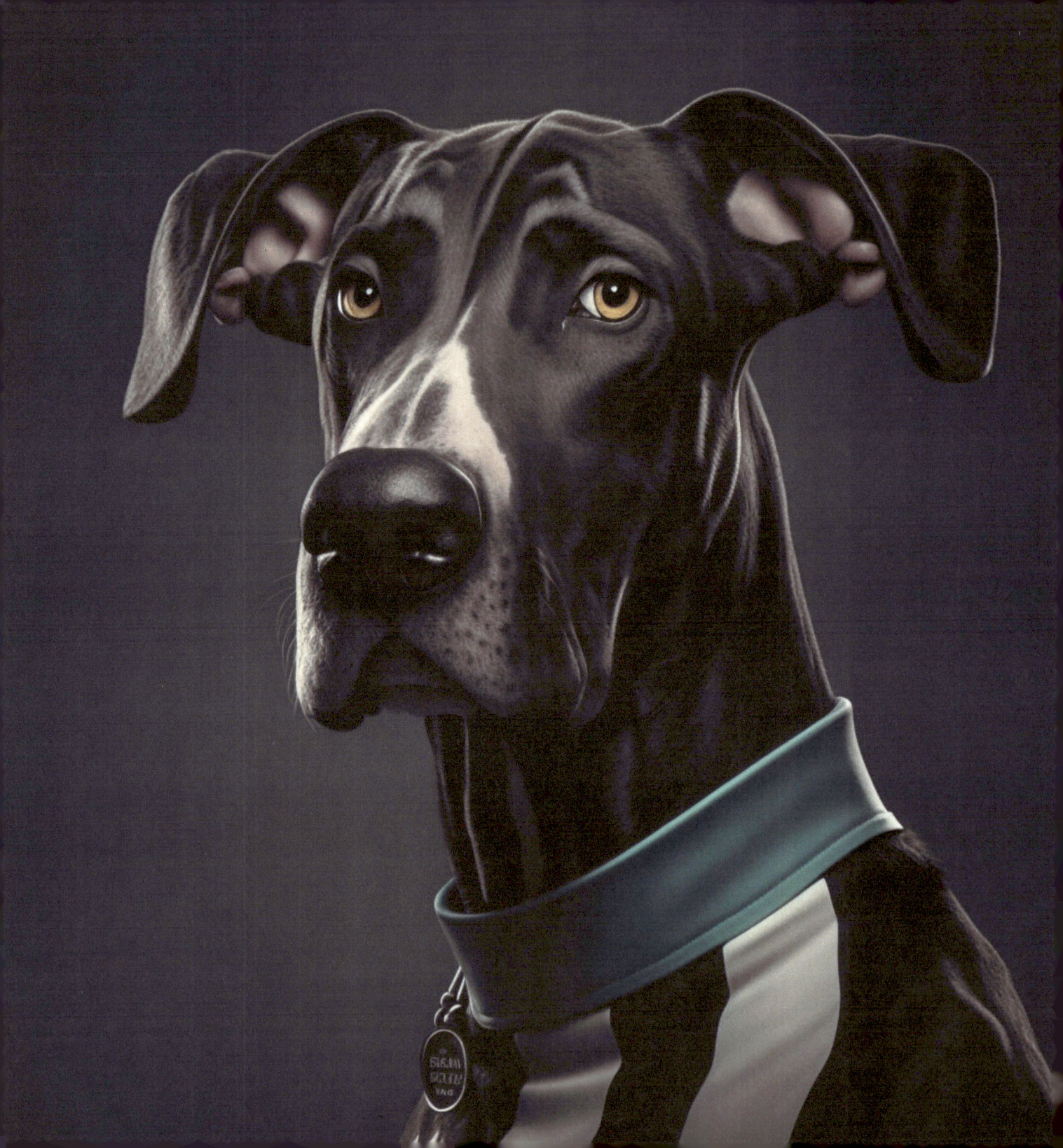

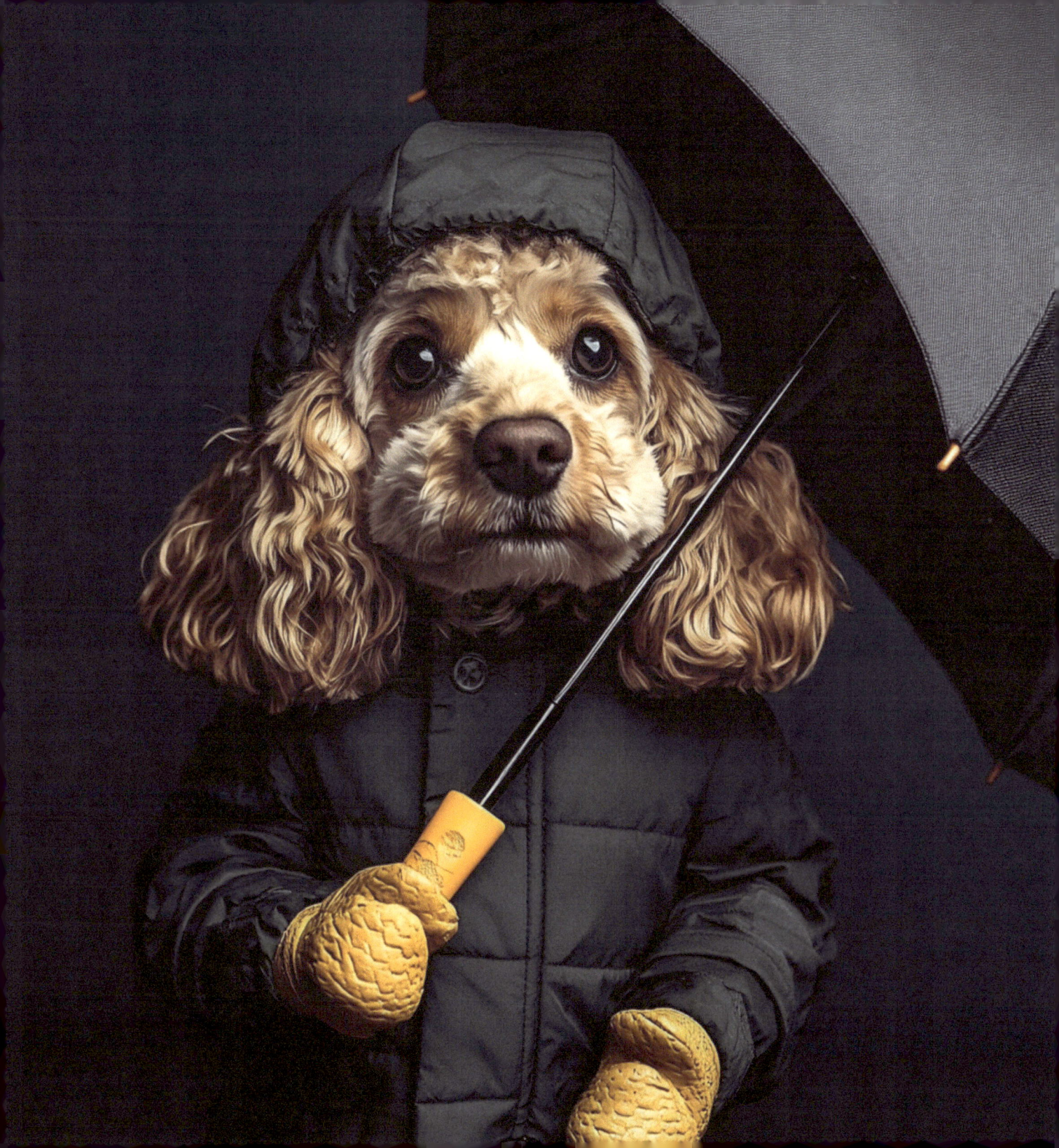

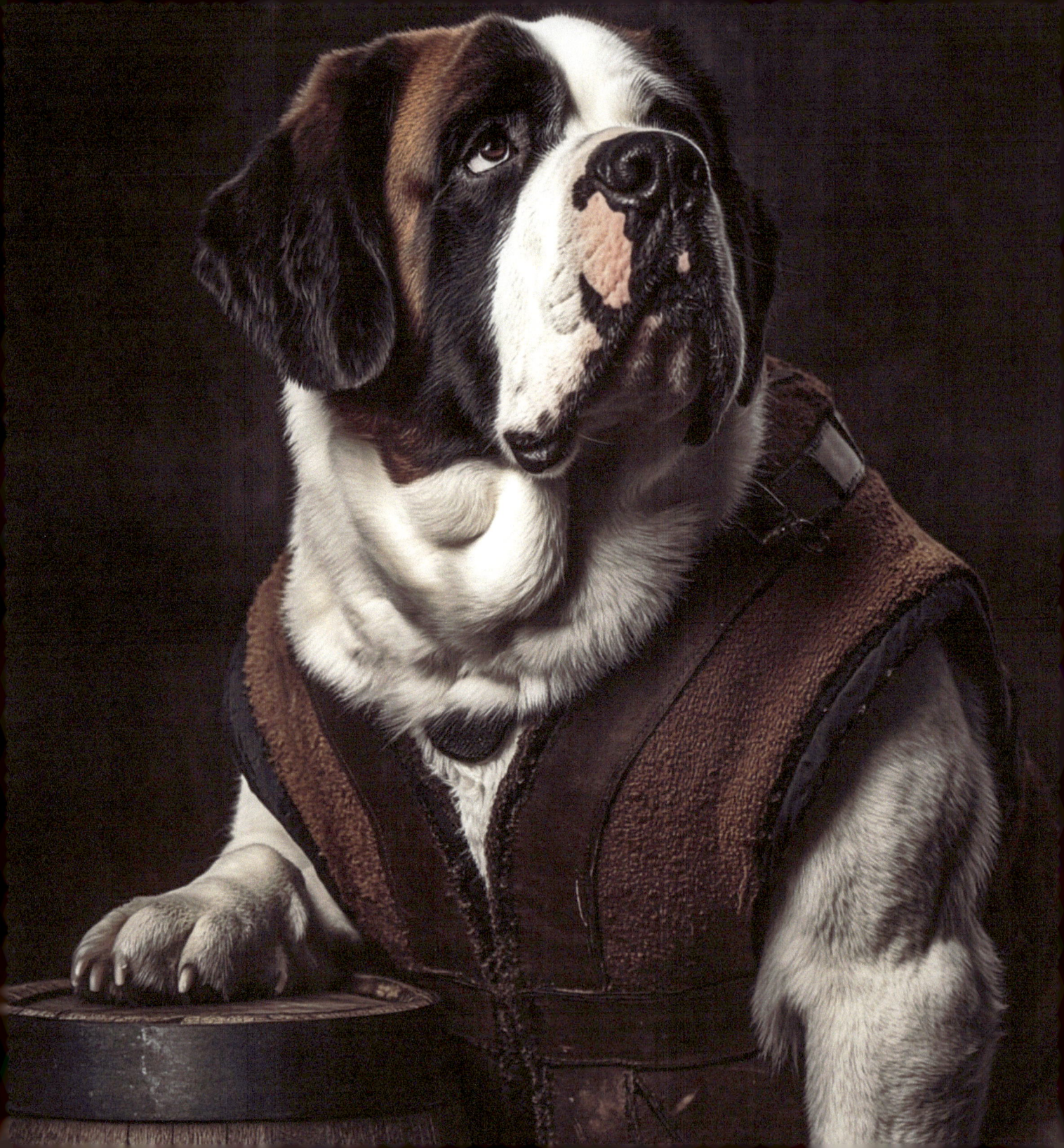

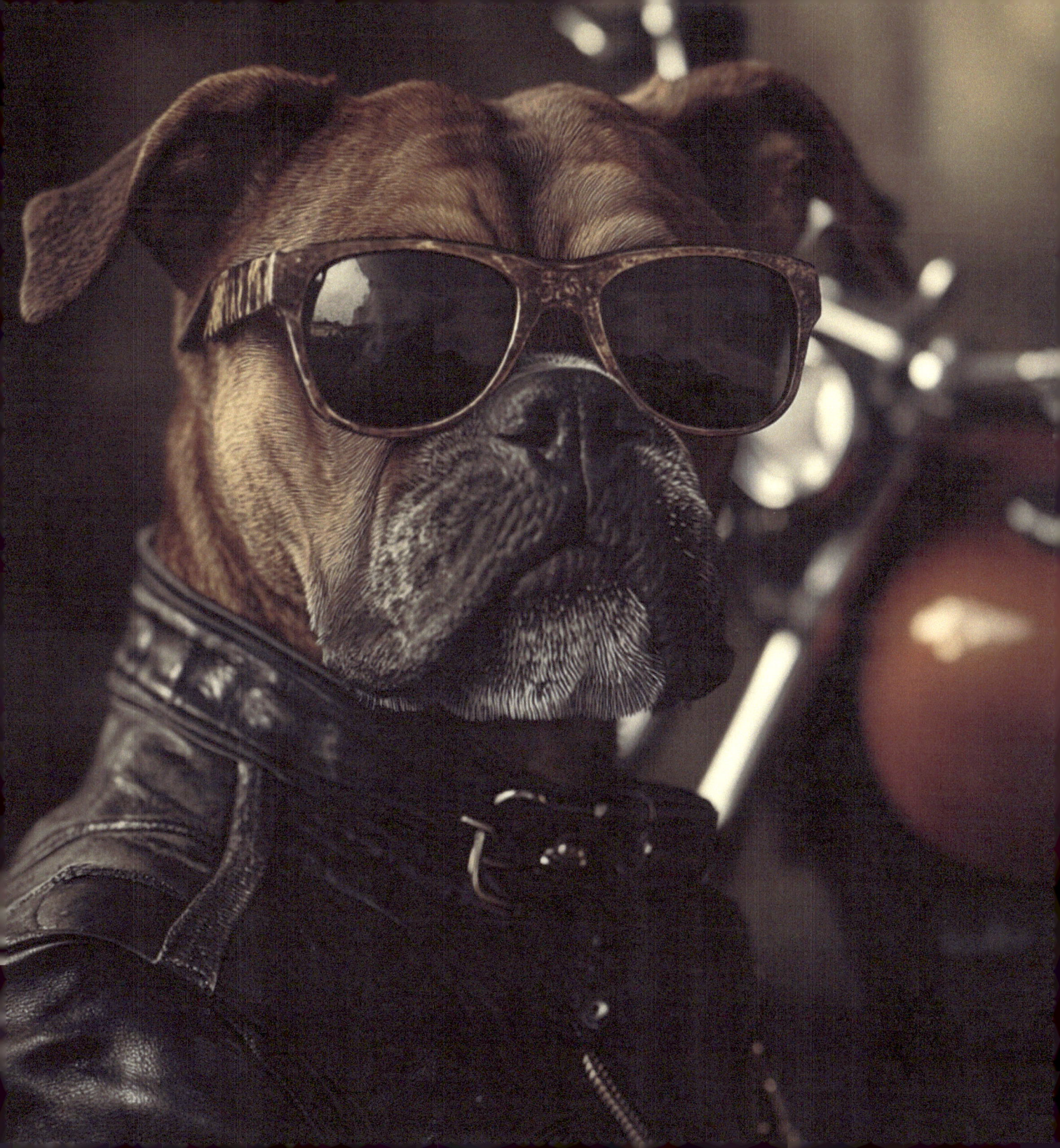

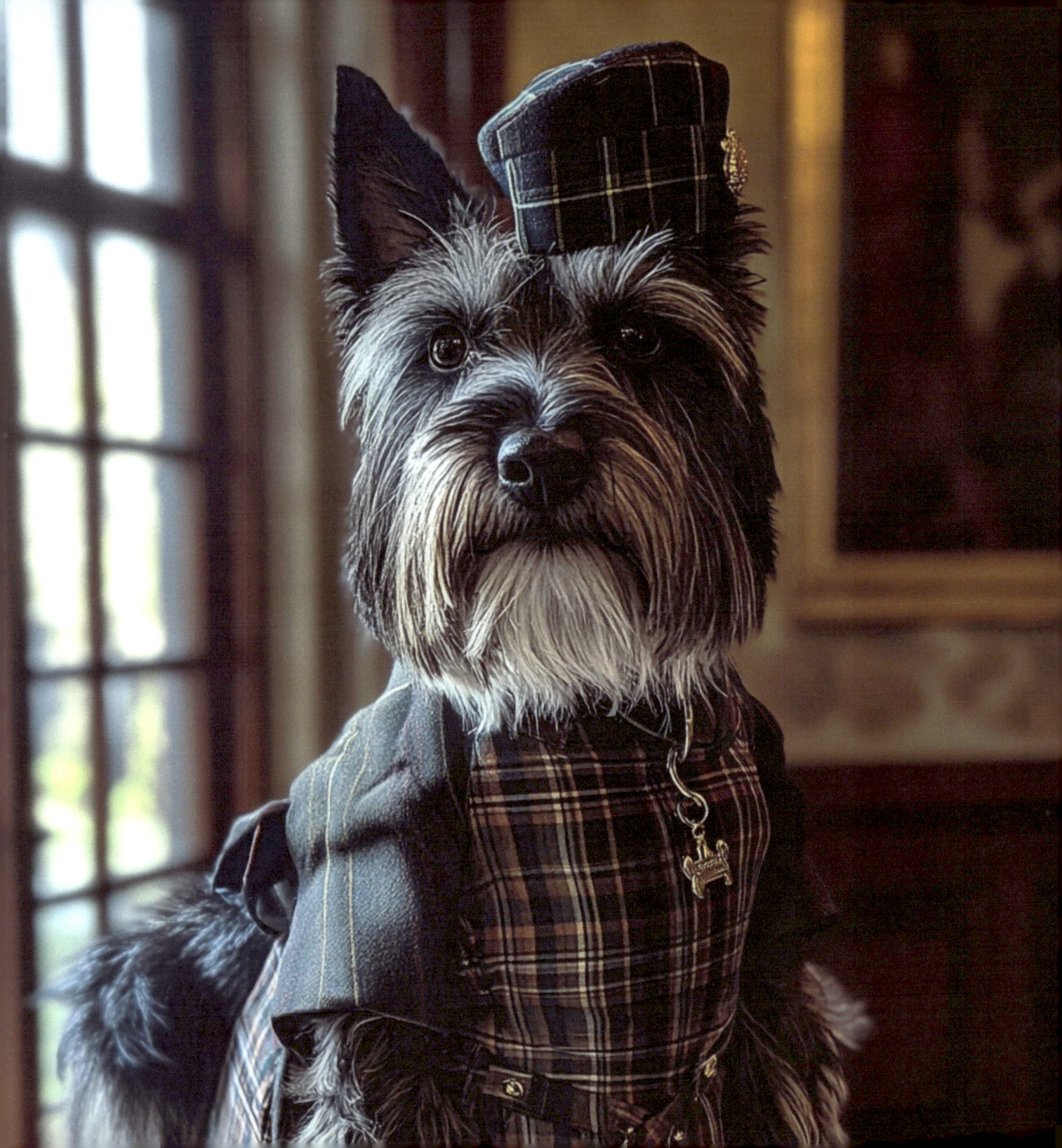

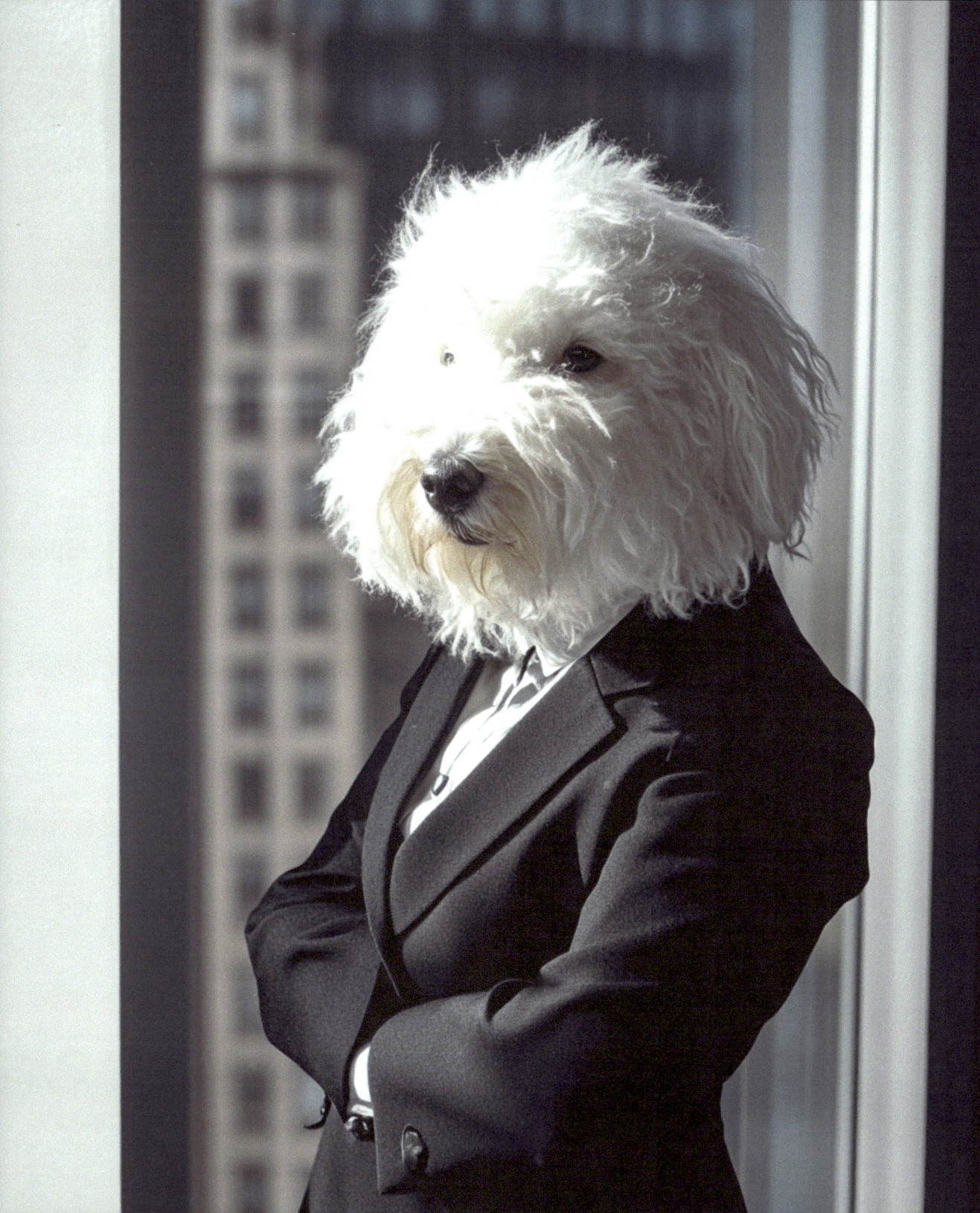

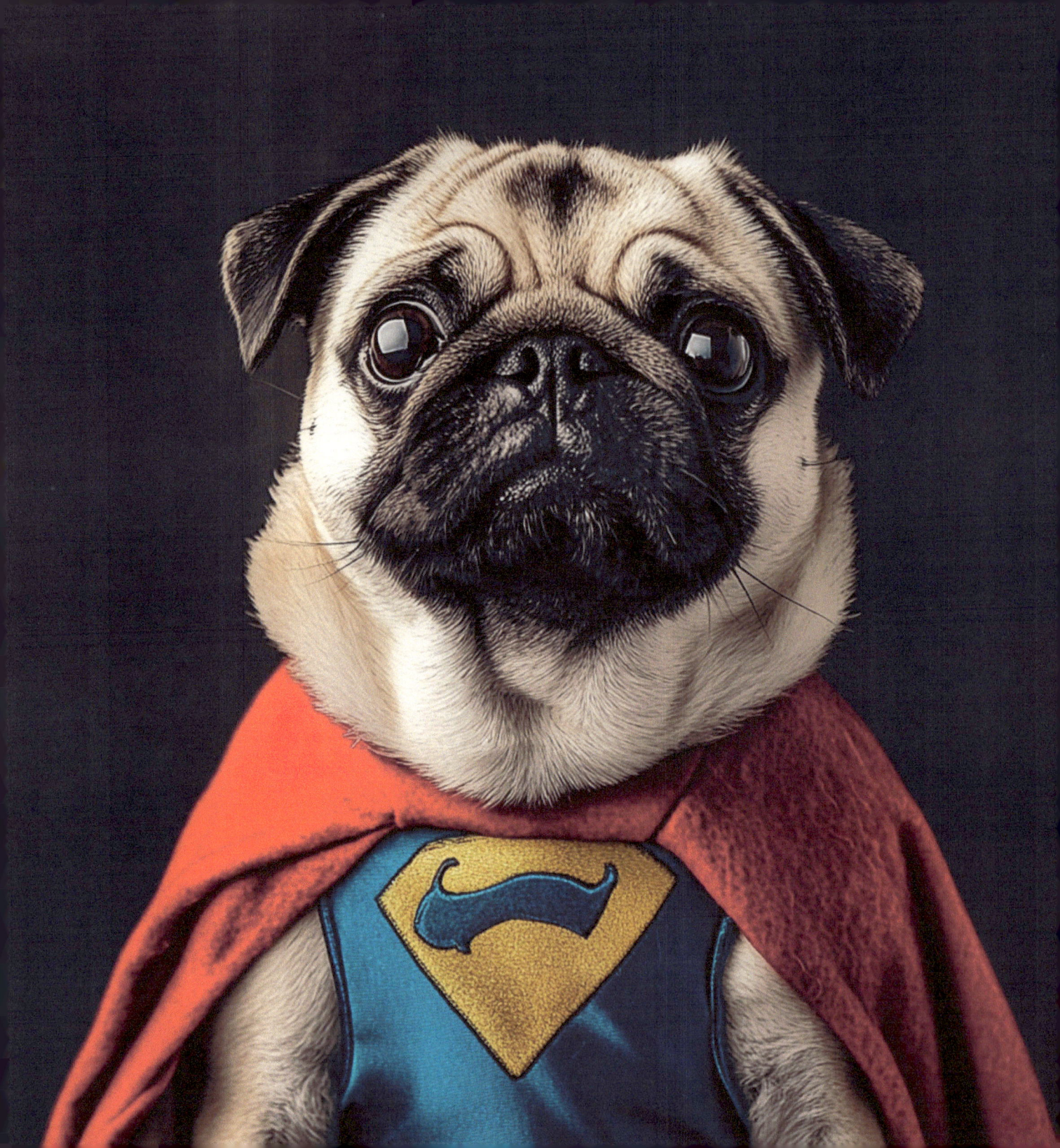

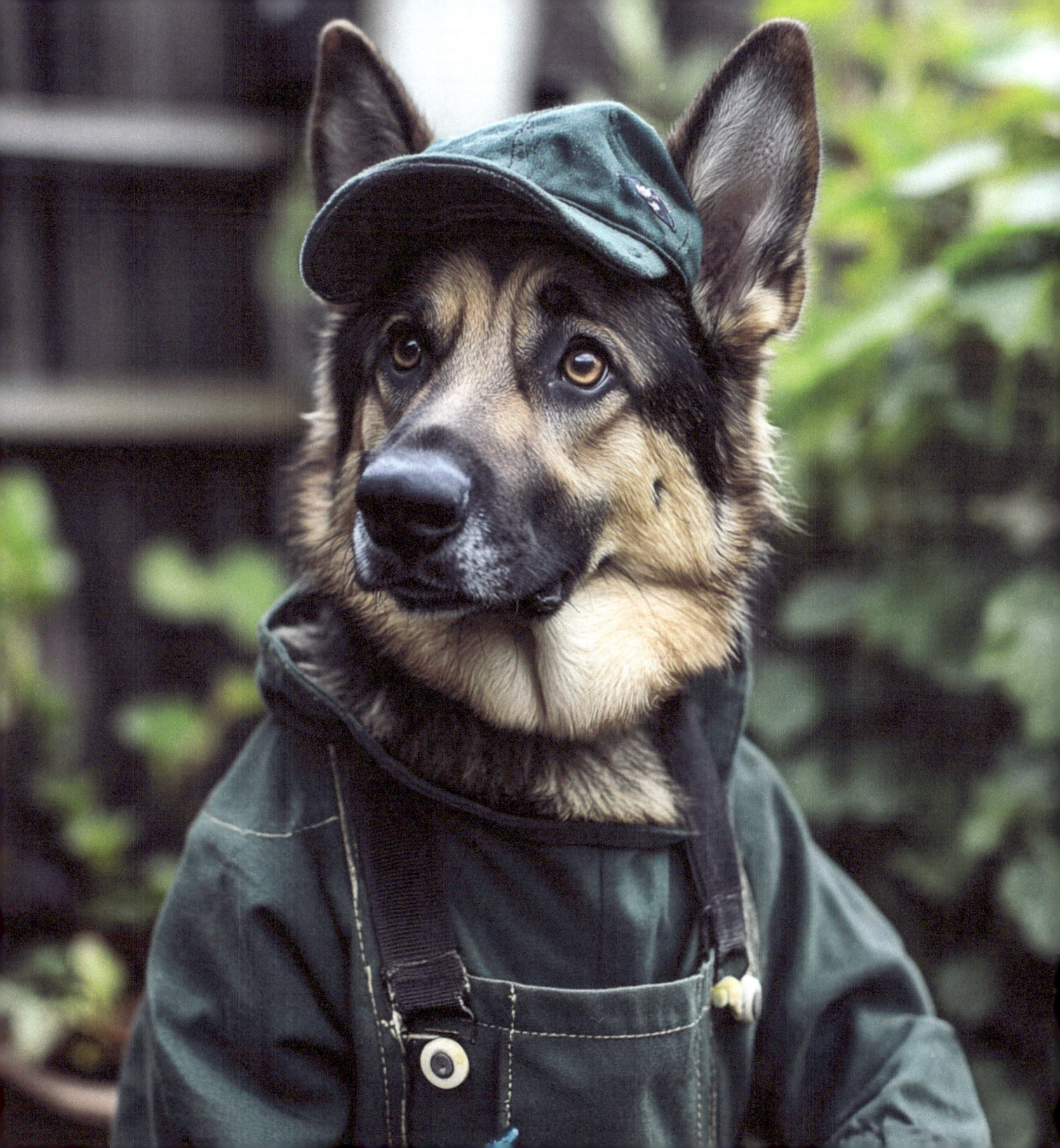

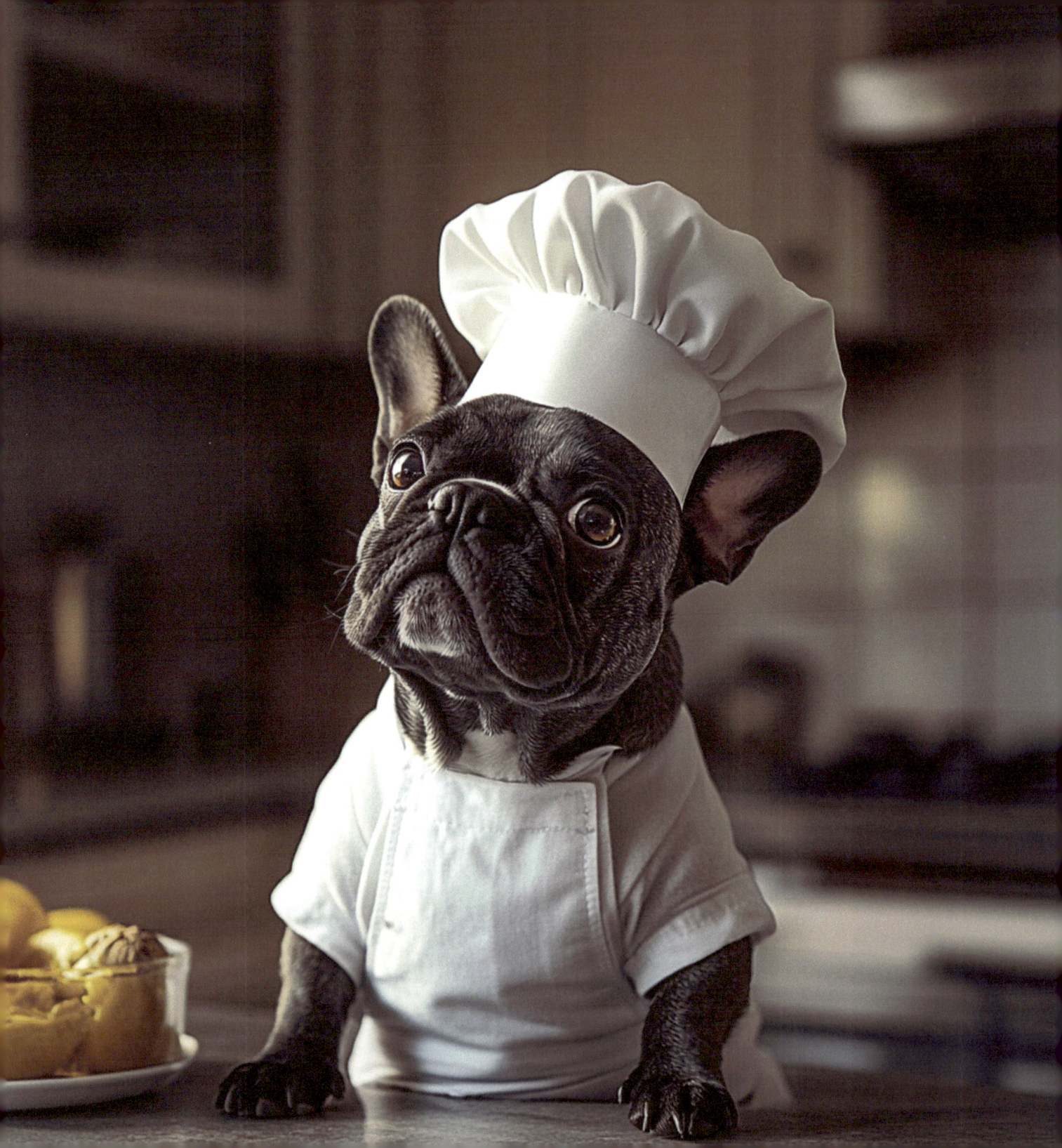

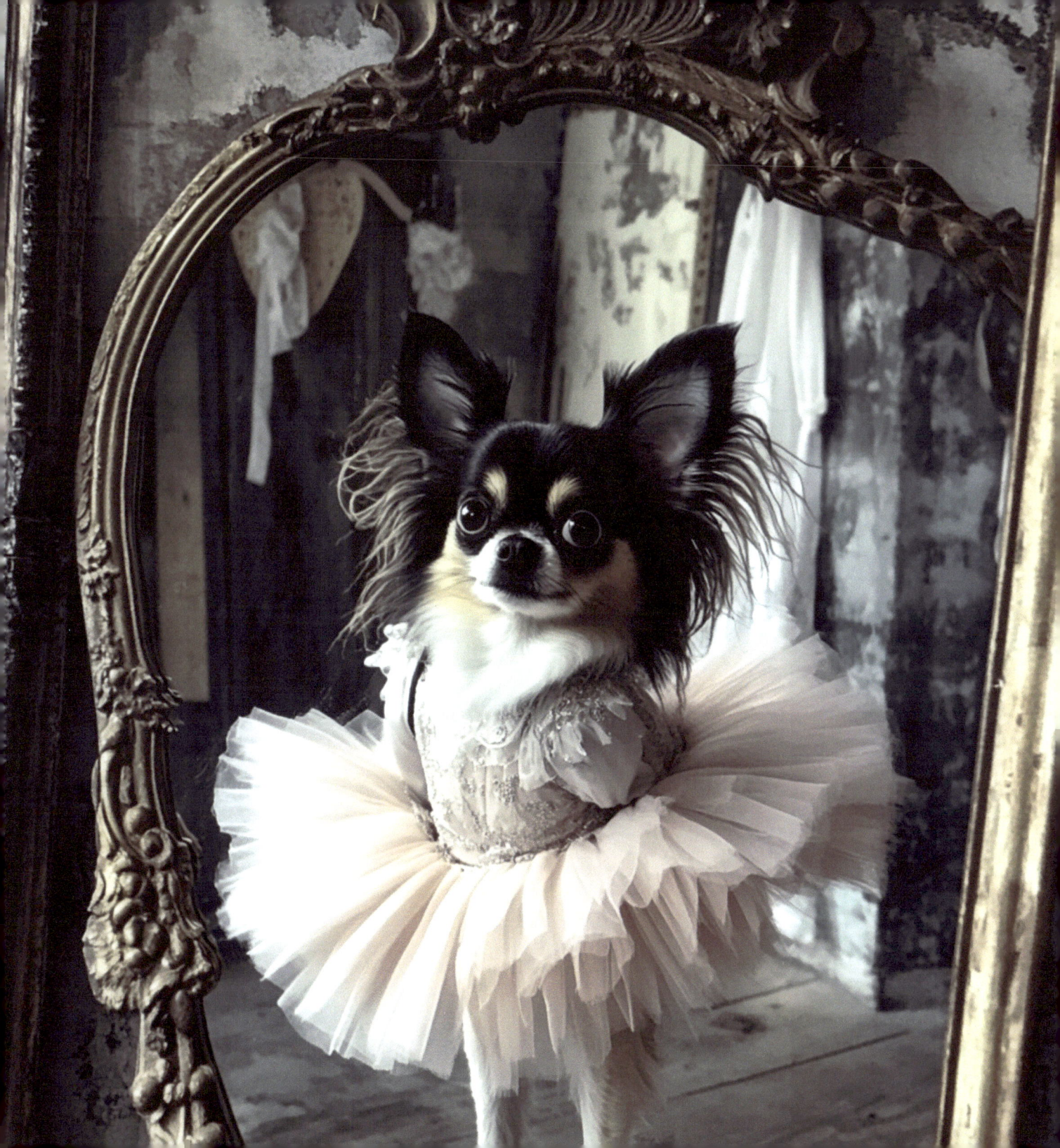

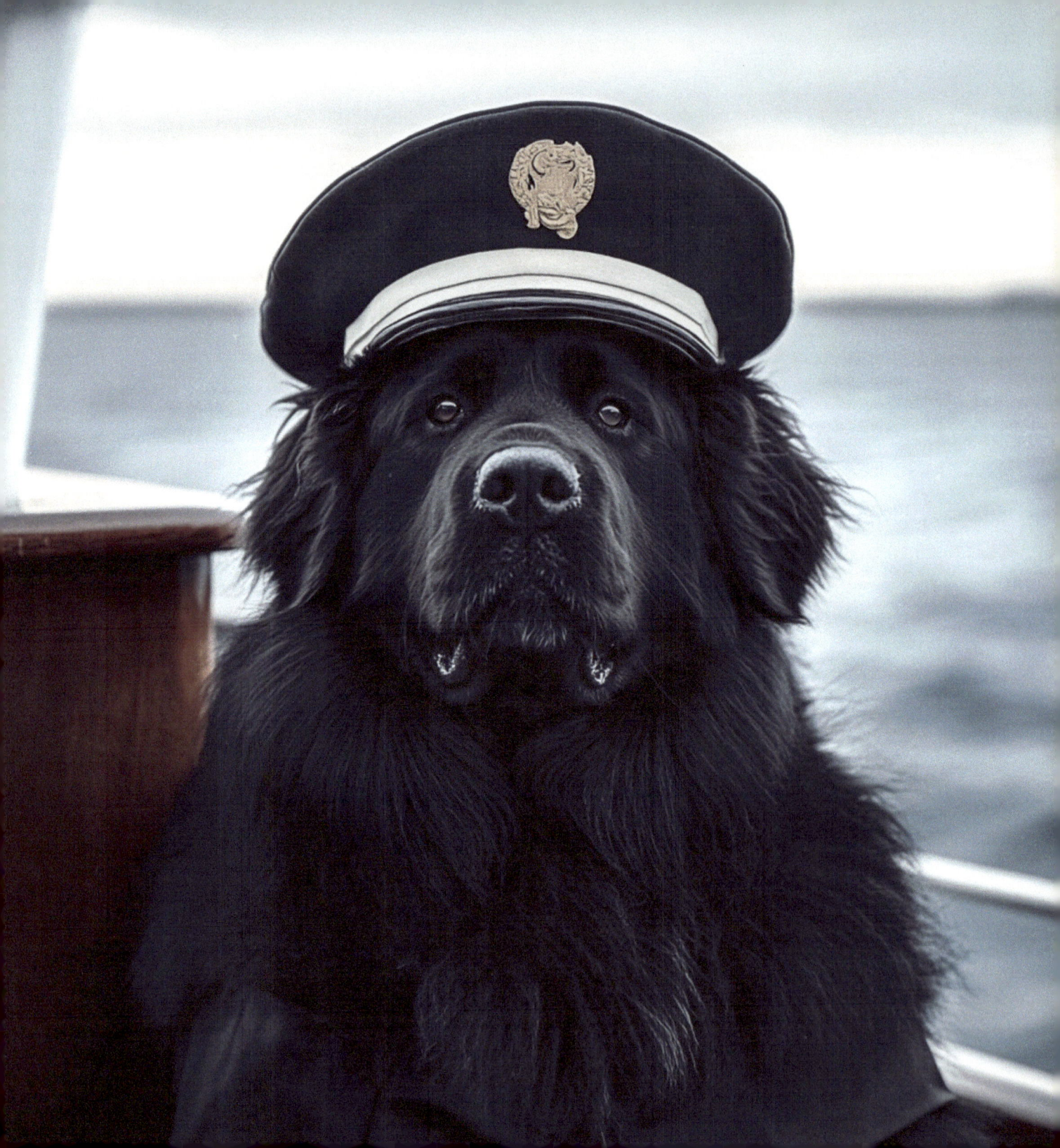

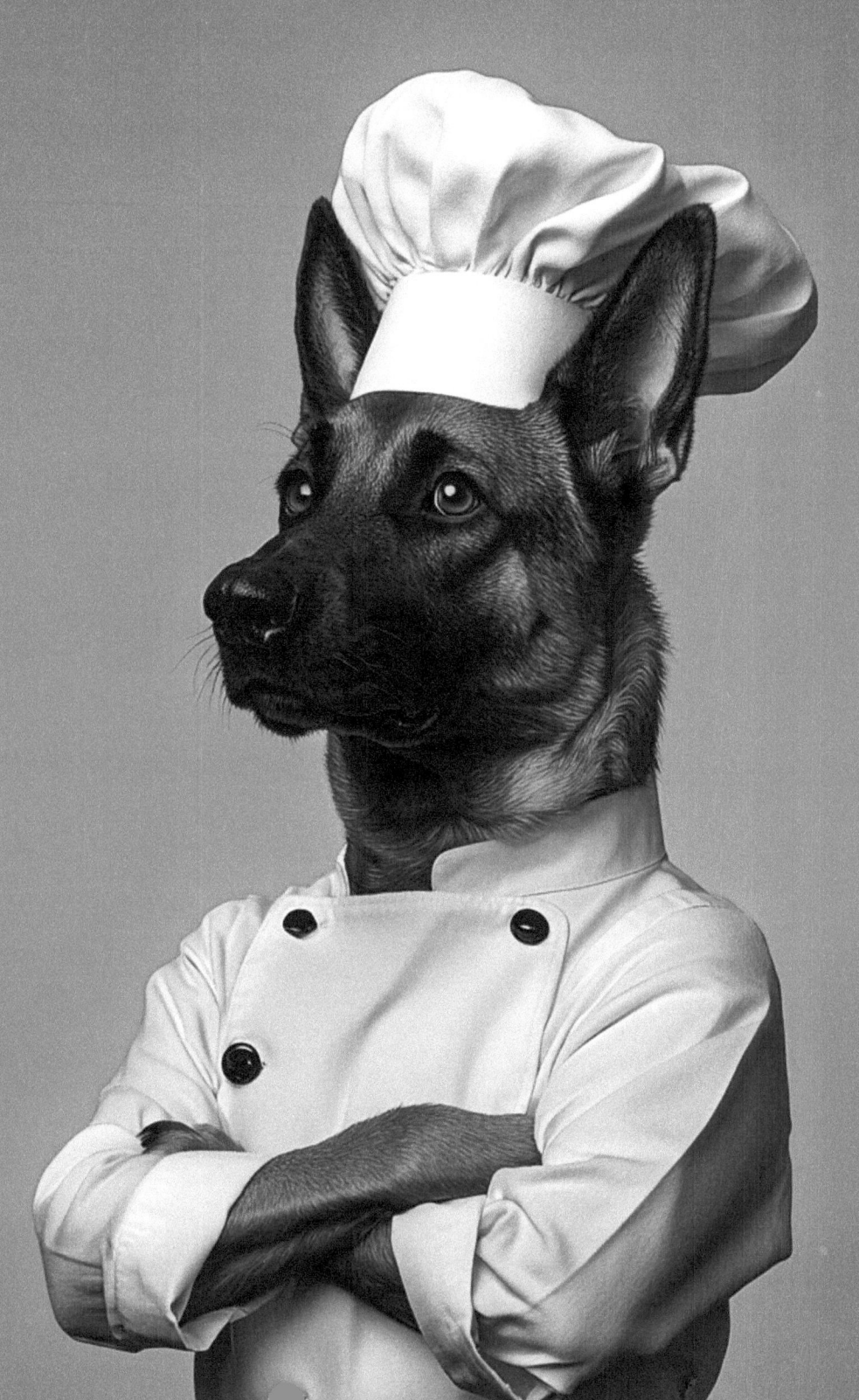

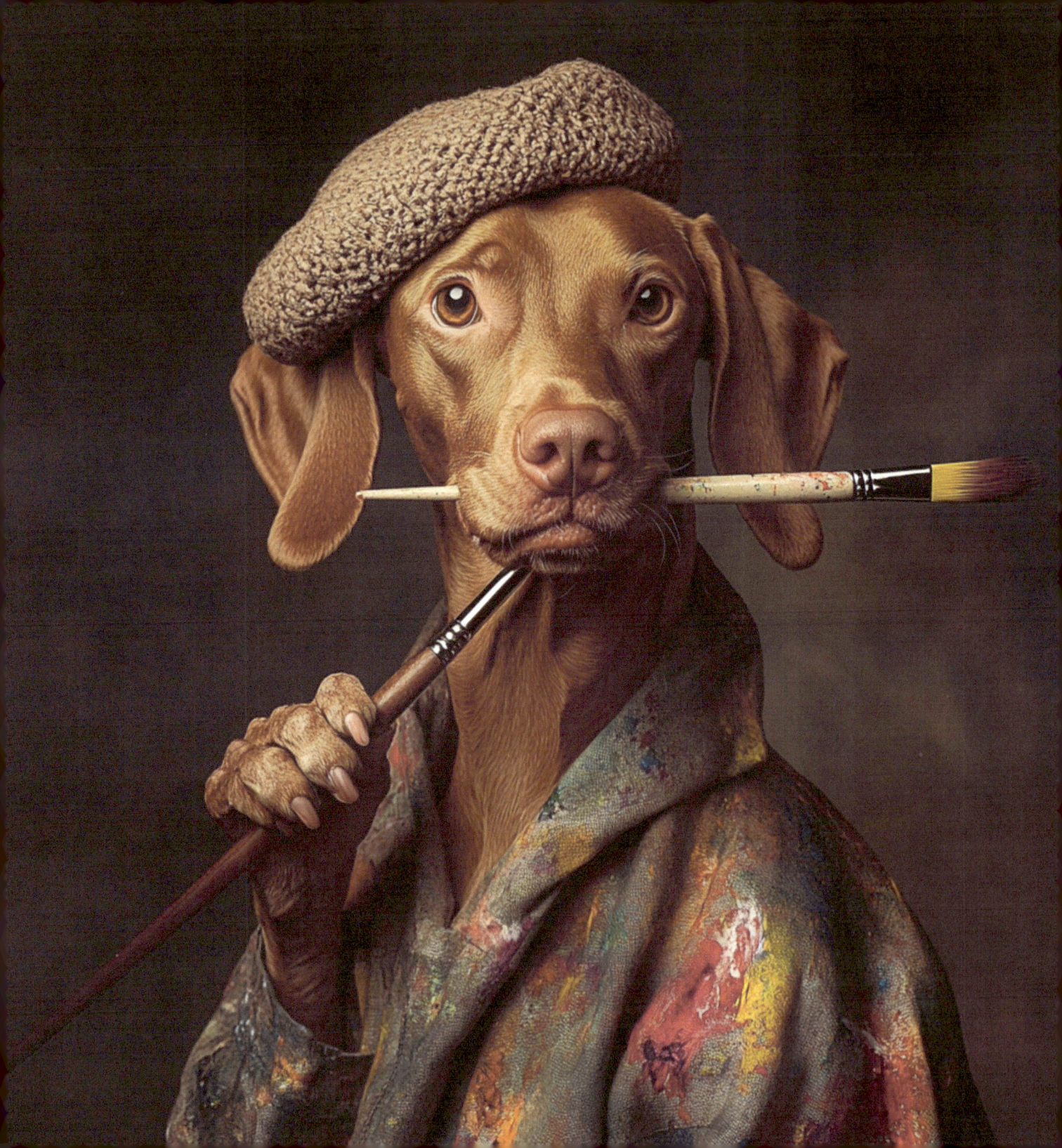

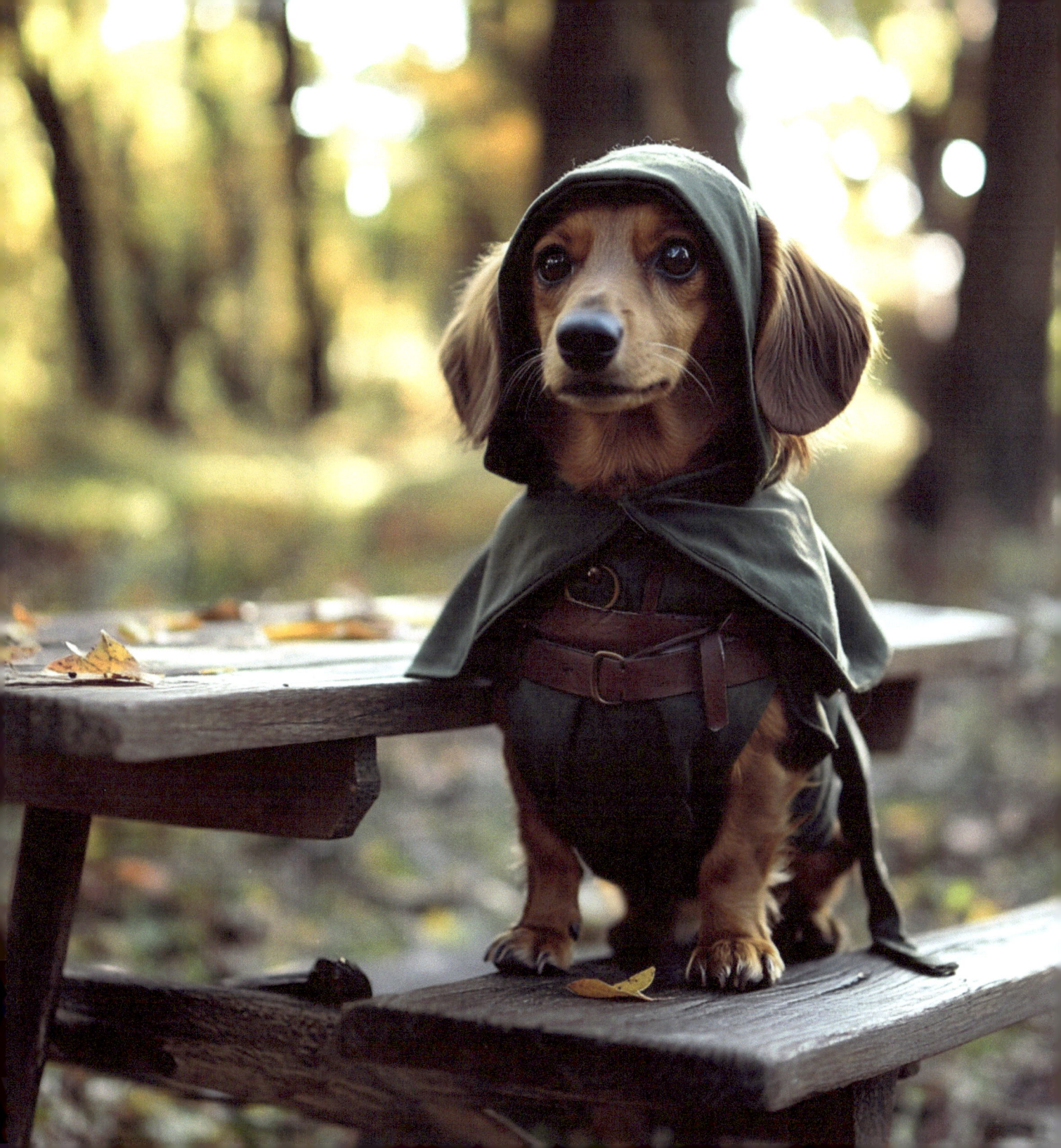

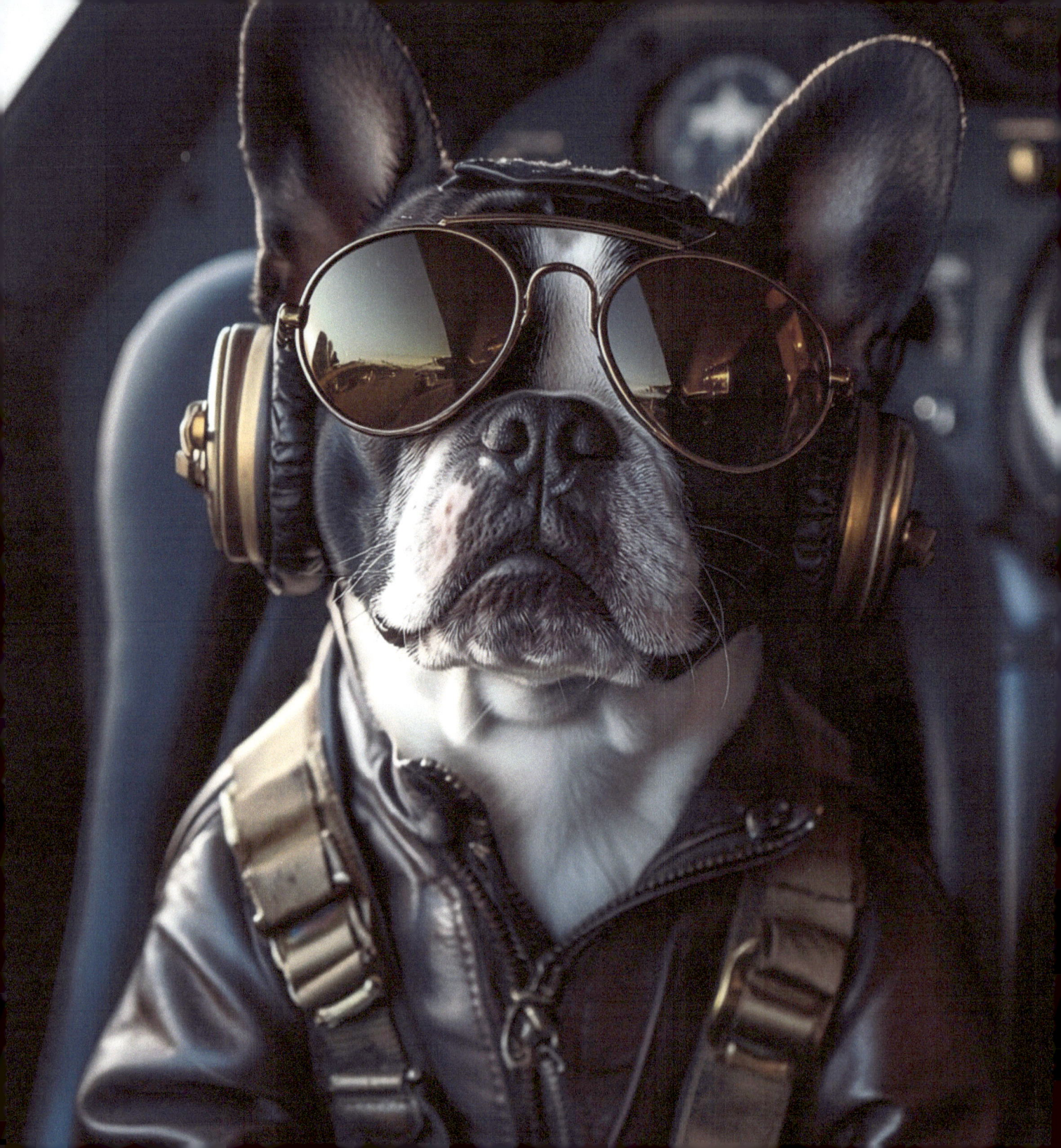

Raeka Harding Picture Books:

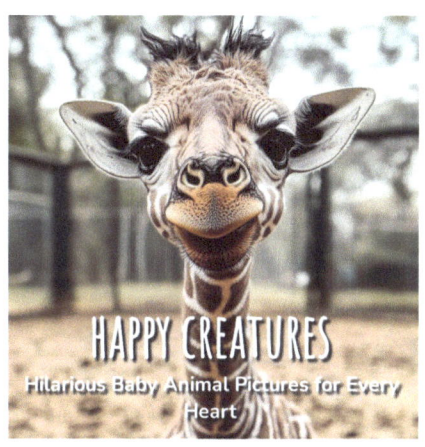 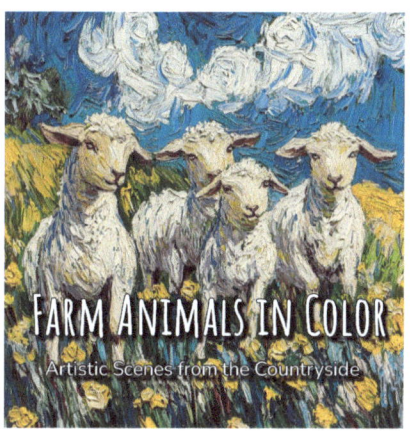 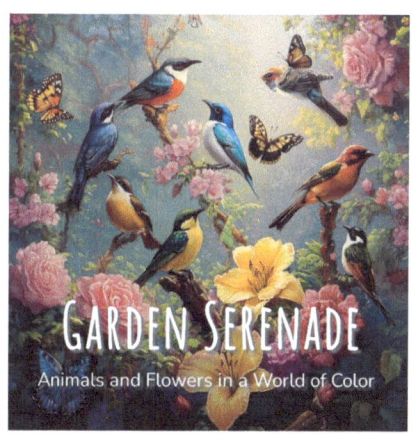

www.ingramcontent.com/pod-product-compliance
Lightning Source LLC
Chambersburg PA
CBHW041933240526
45473CB00034B/1231